Let It Go

*12 New Steps for
Tapping the Power of Your Mind
to Overcome Addiction With FasterEFT*

Let It Go: 12 New Steps for Tapping the Power of Your Mind to Overcome Addiction with FasterEFT

Copyright © 2015 by Marguerite Bonnett

All rights reserved. This book or any portion thereof may not be reproduced or used in any manner whatsoever without the express written permission of the author except for the use of brief quotations in a book review.

ISBN: 978-1512174779

Cover Design: Fiona Jayde, www.FionaJaydeMedia.com

Interior Design: Tamara Cribley, www.DeliberatePage.com

Back cover photograph: LifeTouch. www.LifeTouch.com

Let It Go

*12 New Steps for
Tapping the Power of Your Mind
to Overcome Addiction With FasterEFT*

Marguerite Bonnett

© 2015 Marguerite Bonnett. All rights reserved.

PRAISE FOR *LET IT GO*

"Evidence of Marguerite's great capacity to marry the practice of FasterEFT with the wisdom of 12 step is surpassed only by her innate ability to make the complex simple and the challenging routine. This book is a must have for anyone seriously seeking to successfully take personal power and control of their lives."

~Deirdre Maguire,
FasterEFT Master Practitioner, Author and Speaker

"Marguerite has written a beautiful book that is honest, thought provoking and insightful. Her deep caring and support fill every page. It will change your life for the better, if you let it. It gives you positive and practical tools for transformation that are easy to understand and implement. I highly recommend her book to those committed to continued growth, healing and renewal."

~Rev. Sandy Moore
Minister, InSpirit Center for Spiritual Living Orange County

"Let It Go offers hope to people who have suffered with addictive behaviors. Marguerite Bonnett provides an honest portrayal of her personal life and demonstrates that when real healing takes place, a person's worst nightmare can become their greatest gift. She provides a clear path to releasing old negative beliefs and limitations so we can find inner peace and become the person we've always wanted to be! Marguerite is truly brilliant and inspiring!

~Laura Worley
Advanced FasterEFT Practitioner

"Read this book! Marguerite takes you on an exhilarating ride that empowers your life. Don't resist change; embrace it. Let It Go reveals concrete tools to tap your way to success!"

~Leonard Szymczak, author of *Your GPS Home*

DISCLAIMER:

Because of the dynamic nature of the internet, any web addresses or links contained in this book may have changed since publication and may no longer be valid. The views expressed in this work are solely those of the author and do not necessarily reflect the views of the publisher, and the publisher hereby disclaims any responsibility for them.

The author of this book does not dispense medical advice or prescribe the use of any technique as a form of treatment for physical, emotional, or medical problems without the advice of a physician, either directly or indirectly. The intent of the author is only to offer information of a general nature to help you in your quest for emotional and spiritual well-being. In the event you use any of the information in this book for yourself, which is your constitutional right, the author and the publisher assume no responsibility for your actions.

"Be not conformed to this world: but be ye transformed by the renewing of your mind."

~Romans 12:2

DEDICATION

To Dovell, my beloved husband, the most loving and supportive man I have ever known.

TABLE OF CONTENTS

PREFACE
    TRADITIONAL TWELVE STEPS II
    TWELVE NEW STEPS III

INTRODUCTION
    WHY I CREATED TWELVE NEW STEPS 1

STEP ONE
    TAKE OWNERSHIP 11

STEP TWO
    SEEK WISDOM AND APPLY IT 24

STEP THREE
    DEVELOP INNER COMMUNICATION SKILLS 34

STEP FOUR
    RECOGNIZE THE POWER OF THE MIND/BODY CONNECTION 47

STEP FIVE
    RELEASE THE PAIN AND HURT 57

STEP SIX
    MAKE PEACE INSIDE EVERY MEMORY 64

STEP SEVEN
    FORGIVE EVERYTHING AND EVERYONE 77

STEP EIGHT
    CREATE A MEANINGFUL RELATIONSHIP WITH YOURSELF. 85

STEP NINE
    BECOME NON-JUDGMENTAL 95

STEP TEN
    LIVE FROM NON-ATTACHMENT 101

STEP ELEVEN
    CREATE WITH INTENTIOIN 107

STEP TWELVE
    LIVE WITH PASSION 116

ACKNOWLEDGEMENTS 122

RESOURCE GUIDE 125

BIBLIOGRAPHY 126

ABOUT THE AUTHOR 130

PREFACE

LET IT GO

TRADITIONAL TWELVE STEPS

These are the original twelve steps as published by *Alcoholic Anonymous*:

1. We admitted we were powerless over alcohol-that our lives had become unmanageable.
2. Came to believe that a power greater than ourselves could restore us to sanity.
3. Made a decision to turn our will and our lives over to the care of God as we understood Him.
4. Made a searching and fearless moral inventory of ourselves.
5. Admitted to God, to ourselves, and to another human being the exact nature of our wrongs.
6. Were entirely ready to have God remove all these defects of character.
7. Humbly asked Him to remove our shortcomings.
8. Made a list of all persons we had harmed, and became willing to make amends to them all.
9. Made direct amends to such people wherever possible, except when to do so would injure them or others.
10. Continued to take personal inventory, and when we were wrong, promptly admitted it.
11. Sought through prayer and meditation to improve our conscious contact with God as we understood Him, praying only for knowledge of His will for us and the power to carry that out.
12. Having had a spiritual awakening as the result of these steps, we tried to carry this message to alcoholics, and to practice these principles in all our affairs.[1]

---

[1] Alcoholics Anonymous, Fourth Edition, Alcoholics Anonymous World Services, Inc., New York City, 2001, pages 59-60.

MARGUERITE BONNETT

TWELVE NEW STEPS

These Twelve New Steps were inspired by my study of and work with FasterEFT, the amazing emotional release and belief change technique created by Robert G. Smith.

1. Take Ownership

2. Seek Wisdom And Apply It

3. Develop Inner Communication Skills

4. Recognize The Mind Body Connection

5. Release The Pain And Hurt

6. Make Peace Inside Every Memory

7. Forgive Everyone And Everything

8. Create A Meaningful Relationship With Yourself

9. Become Non-Judgmental

10. Live From Non-Attachment

11. Create With Intention

12. Live With Passion

INTRODUCTION

WHY I CREATED TWELVE NEW STEPS

We are products of our past, but we don't have to be prisoners of it.

~Rick Warren

When I was thirteen, I found my drug of choice–food. It started innocently enough. I was about to enter the eighth grade when my alcoholic stepfather decided the private school I had been attending my whole life was too expensive. So my mother sent me to the Catholic grade school across the street from my house. Eighth grade is a rite of passage, something you graduate from with kids you have spent many years getting to know. Not a party you want to crash at the last minute.

Compared to my previous school, these kids were tough and street smart. I was artistic, sensitive, and about as naïve and sheltered as a child could be. On top of that, my mother was famous; the singing star of TV's Your Show of Shows from 1950-54, star of the Metropolitan Opera, and later, a Vegas headliner. In the 1950's and 60's, when all the big name nightclub performers like Frank Sinatra, Peggy Lee, and Eartha Kitt traveled the circuit of top hotels from New York, to Chicago, Havana (before Castro), Miami, Houston, Los Angeles and of course, Las Vegas, my mother was a major part of that elite group of performers. In my home town of Memphis, Tennessee, that made her the proverbial big fish in the little pond. In 1973, we still appeared to be very rich, despite the fact that my stepfather had already spent a large chunk of my mother's self-made fortune, plunging the family deep into debt. The hippie culture at that time made being rich, or even appearing to be rich, an unforgivable sin, one for which the kids in my new school were determined to make me atone. The boys literally spit on me and the girls were afraid to speak to me for fear of being ostracized.

Since the school was practically across the street from our enormous house, I began sneaking home for lunch, where I watched soap operas and ate massive quantities of whatever food I could find in the pantry. Vienna sausages, canned tamales, creamed soups and crackers became my new friends. When those ran out, I would make a pot of grits and load it up with butter and cheese. Nothing like a heavy Southern meal to lull me into a comatose state so I could survive the afternoon!

As it turned out, my strategy for numbing my emotional pain worked perfectly. It was genius! It was not until months later that I realized all that food caused me to gain weight. A lot of weight. Looking back at childhood pictures, I was a normal sized child, until I compared myself to my younger sister. She was rail thin, so I naturally assumed she was the normal one. At that very young age, I took on the image of myself as fat, wrong and fundamentally flawed. This incorrect thinking, coupled with my unfortunate strategy of eating to sooth emotional pain, set up a pattern of behavior that became a lifelong, ever escalating battle with compulsive overeating.

Fast forward to 2004. After gaining and losing ten pounds, I gained and lost twenty pounds. Then it escalated to the point where I gained and lost thirty, forty, and even seventy pounds! Over my lifetime, I have gained and lost over six hundred pounds. It finally dawned on me that this yo-yo life style was a little insane. Anyone who has experienced any kind of addiction or compulsive behavior will relate to the feeling of losing control, which feels like insanity. What I needed to change was my thinking and my beliefs, not my behavior. But I didn't know that yet.

Trying to change the way I had been living for thirty years challenged me to my core. So, I decided to look for help. That's when I found the twelve step program. I attended my first meeting of Overeaters Anonymous (OA) near my home in California. I walked into that room terrified of admitting I had a problem and joining the ranks of the officially addicted. Inside, the group of mostly women welcomed me with kindness and sympathy. The meeting itself was tightly structured. We read the steps and the traditions out loud. Then, one by one, everyone introduced themselves saying "My name is so-and-so and I *am* a Compulsive Overeater." For some strange reason, the thought of saying those words out loud stung me. At the time, I just assumed that was normal. Hey, I was about to be honest about myself for the first time in decades. That has to be progress, right? I decided to just bite my lip and say it. When they got to me, there was a knot in the pit of my stomach. I told myself, "They're just words. Just say it." I didn't want to disappoint these nice people, so I opened my mouth and out came: "Hi. My name is Marguerite and I *am* a Compulsive Overeater." There, that was not so hard. I told myself that this was a new beginning for me. I knew I had been guided here for a reason, and I decided to stay and listen and learn. The cavalry had arrived! I was finally going to stop this insane behavior and be normal.

During the hour-long meeting, I listened to stories of out-of-control behavior and out of control thinking. Several people in the group had been coming to this same meeting for over fifteen years. That seemed a little odd to me. If they had been thin and eating normally for fifteen years, didn't that mean they were cured? But they claimed a cure was not possible. I would *be* a Compulsive Overeater for the rest of my life. The best I could hope for was to keep coming to the meetings. They said the meetings kept them sane and reinforced their good behavior. However, some in the group were visibly still deeply under the spell of their addiction, despite the regular meetings.

After a month or two of going to meetings, I decided to take the program seriously. I got a sponsor, bought the appropriate reading material, and started to work the steps. I threw myself into it with excitement and a great hope that, at last, I was going to be rid of this mental and physical torment.

One of the tenants of any twelve step program is the idea that there is no healing without a spiritual awakening. No one pushed their particular God on me, which I really appreciated. They simply asked me to get in touch with the "God of my understanding." I grew up with Catholic parents and was cared for by a woman named Becky, a strict Southern Baptist nanny who became my surrogate mother while my own mother travelled around the country performing. I rejected both of those churches as a young adult, so I started looking around for a church that felt good to me.

The first place I found was the Center for Spiritual Living. I'd never heard of Religious Science or New Thought, but I immediately felt at home. It felt more like an empowering philosophy than a traditional religion. My husband had never been interested in any kind of church. But we had recently attended a series of motivational seminars and I convinced him to come with me by calling it our "Sunday Seminar." The minister's talks every Sunday touched me deeply. I had never experienced such a strong feeling of loving acceptance and non-judgment anywhere in my life. I was embarrassed that I could not stop the tears streaming down my face every Sunday as I listened to the messages of New Thought spirituality. Just weeks later, I decided to take their foundations class and that decision forever altered my perspective and my life.

Meanwhile, with the help of my OA sponsor, I made it to Step Four: "taking a searching and fearless moral inventory." I was given eleven typed pages of directions, complete with one hundred and seventy essay questions divided into three sections: childhood, adolescence, and adulthood. The questions felt very one sided and seemed structured to bring up every negative circumstance and emotion I had ever felt or experienced. Here's a sampling of the questions, to give you an idea of the intensity:

Childhood:
- Describe what you think your family thought of you.

- How did your parents punish you?

- List all the feelings of guilt, fear, resentment you had toward each person in your life as a child.

- Did your appearance embarrass you?

Adolescence:
- Did you feel you were a coward because you didn't want to fight? Or did you like to fight? Were you a bully? Did you feel embarrassed because anyone made fun of you or avoided you?

- First sexual intercourse, what were your feelings? Did you feel guilty? Disappointed? Be as explicit about the feelings as you can.

- List in detail any homosexual experiences, masturbation fantasies, any other sexual activity you particularly remember … keep in mind that we are not concerned about who with, when or on what date, or how often, but rather how did you feel about the experience?

- Did you have the kind of clothes that other kids wore? Was there enough money for the things that you needed and if not, were you resentful of that? If there was, did you take it for granted? Did you feel any sibling got more than you did? Write out your feelings about money as an adolescent.

Adulthood:

- When, how and in just what instances did my selfish pursuit of sex relations damage other people and me? What people were hurt and how badly? Did I spoil my marriage and injure my children? Did I jeopardize my standing in the community?

- If you have married a cold, unloving person, ask yourself why you chose that person to be your mate. Did you use it as an excuse to find new romances? Was your mother or father cold and unloving and is this your chance to get even with them through your spouse?

- Are you still a baby in your parents' eyes and take advantage of this?

- Do you gossip about others?

- Do you feel the world owes you a living?

- If revenge were possible right now, who would be the top people on your list? Why?

- What is your greatest fear?

- Do you feel you somehow have to prove that you are worthy of love from others, either here or elsewhere? Elaborate on this.[2]

Just reading these questions made me feel queasy. Having to answer all 170 of them in a "searching and fearless" way was debilitating. It took me almost a month to complete them, at the end of which I was nearly suicidal. "Searching" for answers to negative questions was focusing my attention and enlarging the experience of every painful, fearful, and sad moment in my life. There was not one single question about any positive thing that had ever happened to me.

Suddenly, I was feeling bad about my marriage. I could not find anything good about my new beautiful house I had so lovingly decorated and landscaped. I became so depressed that I sought out a psychiatrist. His only tool to help me consisted of putting me on Prozac. I went from having a problem using food to soothe myself to swimming in a sea of emotional excrement, and eating pills to keep me from drowning. How was this supposed to help?

Back at the Center for Spiritual Living, I learned about the power of the mind and the nature of God. The Center also taught me that what I focus on grows bigger and tends to show up in my life. And to find God, I must look within, not outside of myself. In fact, God is the Source and Perfection of all that is, including me. So if God is perfect, and I am a creation of God, then at the level of my Essence, I would have to be perfect, too. It's the ego that identifies with outside objects and situations. It was my ego that was identifying with my challenge

---

[2] *An Abstinence Model For Compulsive Eaters: Honesty, Openmindedness, Willingness (H.O.W.) Sponsor's Guideline,* Published by CALOA, Revised March 1995, Reprinted May 15, 1995, Fourth Step Inventory-General Guidelines, pages 11-21

of compulsive overeating. A compulsive overeater is not *who I am.* I am a child of God. I am a spiritual being having a human experience. One of those human experiences may be overeating. But that is not who I am. What a relief! These ideas just felt true to me. And if these were the basics of Religious Science, I wanted to know more.

At the moment of this new revelation, I had finally finished my searching and fearless moral inventory and was told I must read it out loud to my sponsor. That's Step Five: "Admit to God, ourselves and to another human being the exact nature of our wrongs." It took several sessions over several days. I cried through half of it, wanting to stop. But my sponsor encouraged me to continue, reassuring me that I had indeed been a *victim* of much pain in my life. It was no wonder I had an obsessive compulsion. She even told me that my life had been tougher than hers! I actually felt that she enjoyed my painful stories far more than she should have. I wonder now if I misjudged her simply because I was spiraling down into an emotional abyss of my own making.

Another part of me wanted to complete this Step Five ordeal; to finish; to let it go. However, reading the list made it bigger and more real than writing it. At the time, I could not understand how I had ever survived what had become my horrific life. I thought if I had to live with all this negativity, I'd really rather be dead.

In therapy, I was led to believe that knowing *why* I was depressed would help me to heal. Well, I finally knew, in excruciating detail, exactly why I was depressed and overeating. Or so I thought. I'll be the first to admit, I do not have a degree in psychiatry or any kind of cognitive therapy. However, speaking from personal experience, knowing the source of my depression did absolutely *nothing* to alleviate it. And neither did the drugs! In fact, I was more depressed than I had ever been in my entire life.

With a sliver of hope, I pushed on to Step Six: "Were entirely ready to have God remove all these defects of character," and Step Seven: "Humbly asked Him to remove my shortcomings." That brought me back around to prayer.

At the Center for Spiritual Living, Religious Science was redefining not only how I prayed, but the very nature of the God I was praying to. Up to that point, God was a somewhat frightening figure who existed outside of me and made things happen to me. This relationship to God created a victim consciousness and a feeling of powerlessness. The traditional Step One is "We admitted we were powerless over [some addiction] – that our lives had become unmanageable." I had indeed embodied that point of view. I felt powerless in all areas of my life. So it was quite a revelation to learn that God is within me and in every person, place, situation and thing, and there are spiritual laws that I can use to effect change in my life. I found this new philosophy extremely exciting. While it intellectually felt right and good to me at the time, I now know that I had only just scratched the surface of a deep spiritual awakening that would take time and effort to fully embody.

My twelve step meetings became more and more difficult to sit through. My sponsor suggested I become a sponsor to a newcomer, and I did. But when this new twelve stepper balked at the program, I could not honestly guide her to do what I had done, and she left. I began to question the program out loud, which was not welcomed. My sponsor got tougher and more impatient with me as I struggled with holding the paradox of these two philosophies in my heart and mind. Finally, I had to choose. New Thought won my heart and mind. I left the group and my sponsor.

Secretly, I missed the group. Actually, I did not miss the group. I missed the connections I'd made with several of the women in the group. But we were not allowed to socialize outside the meetings or even say "Hello" at the grocery. That might put the other person in a compromising position if they were with someone and they did not want to explain our connection. I am the type of person who sees a friend at the grocery and wants to rush over and give them a hug! But I respected the program's traditions. Still, I longed for a supportive group of people with whom I could share my journey.

My new journey was no longer one of "recovery," but one of un-covering Who I Really Am, the true nature of my being, and my relationship to God. I prayed for guidance until one day I heard a voice inside me say, "Why don't you write your own twelve step program?" I immediately went to work on that and as I did, the Universe began to reconfigure itself around my new intention.

A conspiracy of fortunate events magically presented themselves to me, practically forcing me to write this book and forever change my life. One of those fortunate events was finding FasterEFT, the phenomenal tapping modality that enabled me to release the underlying causes of my behavior. As I trained to become a practitioner, I began to weave the FasterEFT belief system into my twelve new steps. I initially developed these twelve new steps for my own personal reference and well being.

They are both powerful and sensible. And they create peace and freedom. I believe I have found the key to peace on Earth. World peace will exist when there is peace *inside* every individual. I have made it my life's mission to help create that peace, one person at a time.

It is not my intention to label any program, twelve step or otherwise, good or bad. I have simply recounted my personal experience with one such group. I know several individuals for whom a twelve step program saved their lives. I know others who belong to twelve step programs that celebrate their sobriety in an empowering and uplifting way; even FasterEFT practitioners and members of Centers for Spiritual Living. I believe that if it is working for you, keep doing it. And, it is my intention and my life's purpose to serve those who are not being served by other programs or who simply need a little extra help letting go of their old patterns. Page fifty-eight of the Big Book of Alcoholics Anonymous says, "Some of us have tried to hold on to our old ideas and the result was nil until we let go absolutely."[3] Some might call FasterEFT an "easier, softer way" to let it go. And they would be correct. It may be faster and easier, but FasterEFT tapping requires complete honesty and a degree of fearlessness. You still have to go back to the painful memories and see, hear, and feel them for the last time. But once you learn how to truly LET IT GO, you open the door to miracles.

In January of 2015, I went to Habilitat Drug and Alcohol Treatment Center in Hawaii as part of a team offering FasterEFT sessions to their long term residents. While Habilitat gives people the life skills they never learned because of their early addiction to drugs, FasterEFT provides them with something no other program has ever given them: the opportunity to release the painful emotional drivers that caused them start using and kept them using. Once the emotional drivers are uncovered and released, we then used FasterEFT to create a negative association to their drug, virtually eliminating all desire for their previous "addiction." The results were so astounding they cemented in me the belief that we are not our behavior. And anyone can become free of any addiction.

FasterEFT tapping is an easy and effective tool that keeps me not only sane, but constantly growing into new levels of peace, joy, health, and prosperity.

---

3   Alcoholics Anonymous, Fourth Edition, Alcoholics Anonymous World Services, Inc., New York City, 2001, page 58.

There is scientific proof that real change is possible now. You are *not* your behavior. You are so much more than that. And once you understand how behavior is created, you will be empowered to make the deep changes you desire, which will reveal the truth of Who You Really Are and change your whole world in the process.

I invite you to step into the life you were meant to live. The Twelve *New* Steps laid out in this book walk you through a healing journey that connects you to inner resources you didn't even know you had. Climbing out of the abyss does not have to be so hard. The power is inside you right now. It is my great honor and privilege to be your guide.

STEP ONE

TAKE OWNERSHIP

If you own the story, you get to write the ending.

~Brené Brown

For years, I confused personal shame and blame with taking ownership. I claimed my helplessness and worthlessness and wore it like a badge of honor. I believed there was something fundamentally wrong with me and no matter how hard I tried, I could never fix it. And as I held that belief, my life expressed helplessness and worthlessness in so many ways. Until I learned the truth.

Step One asks you to own whatever is going on in your life. This is *your* life! It is not mine, not your parents, not your boss's and not your partner's. It's yours. This does not mean you have to tell a bunch of stories about what you've done or what has been done to you.

There is nothing broken about you because there are no broken people. Some of you may be thinking, "But you don't know me or the things I've done. I'm very broken and I can't imagine how anyone could fix me. Not even God wants to fix me."

I've had similar thoughts, and I have worked with clients who felt so bad they wished they were dead. People learn how to hurt themselves. And some learn how to hurt others. I use the word "learn" intentionally. A person does not suddenly decide to become a monster.

In my experience, trauma either happened to them, or it was modeled for them at a young age.

I met a man recently who was carrying guilt, sadness, and self-loathing about getting caught when he was eight years old doing something sexually inappropriate to another child. His family labeled him "sick" and "horrible." In his thirties, he still carried those labels and was not welcome at family gatherings. He expressed hatred for himself, saying "What kind of a sick person does that?" During a FasterEFT session, a memory surfaced of him at four years old being left with the neighbor's kids. They were doing the exact same inappropriate behavior to him. He was hurt, afraid, and confused. Clearly, the behavior was learned. It had been done to him and his child mind had no idea what to do with that experience, so it expressed itself as a behavior.

This man grew up to be a social activist, working tirelessly helping others, while constantly punishing himself inside. He spent his life trying to make up for this horrible behavior that he could not explain. When he decided to stop the shame and blame and take real ownership of his past, he found a way to heal it using FasterEFT. By healing his past, he made himself an even greater activist and compassionate helper.

Taking ownership is not about focusing on how messed up and powerless you are. In fact, it's quite the opposite. You are far from powerless.

You are so much more than your behavior. At the very center of your being, at the level of your Essence, you are pure. Pure potential. Pure energy. Pure Love. You are an individualized expression of the Infinite Creativity of the Universe.

When you take ownership, you embrace your power!

Embracing your power involves understanding Who You Really Are. When you understand how the mind works, you realize that every second of your life is an opportunity for choice. The quality of the choices you make in every moment is born from the beliefs you carry around inside you. Based on your life experience, you made decisions which ultimately became your beliefs. The stories you tell about your life define your "truth." This book will explain in great detail how that works.

I have worked with people who suffer from addictions of all kinds. The one thing they all seem to have in common is some sort of traumatic past experience. In other words, there is a reason they are addicted. Their emotional pain is so severe that it drives them to find a way to escape their pain, at any cost. I have also worked with clients who have experienced such severe childhood abuse that their mind blocked it out completely, until something happened. For one client, it was the day her daughter reached the age when she was first abused. Her memories came screaming back, and her life went into a tail spin as she tried to cope with these "new" memories.

From the point of view of your unconscious mind, addiction is a success. Addictions are coping mechanisms. You had a problem, and you did something. Maybe you took it, shot it up, drank it, ate it, bought it, watched it, had sex with it, or gambled it. Whatever you did, for a little while, you managed to forget about all those painful emotions. You escaped. You felt better. Or at least you were distracted, even if it was only for a little while. To your unconscious mind, that was a success. So your unconscious mind filed it under "That worked!"

The next time you felt bad, your unconscious mind remembered the behavior that made the bad feelings go away and you did it again. Eventually, that addictive behavior was repeated enough times that it became hard wired into your neurology, and Voila, you installed a program! Now, you find it impossible *not* to do it because it runs on automatic pilot. You can have a cigarette, a drink, a drug, a brownie or a mouse in your hand before you are even aware you are doing it. I've been there.

The good news is, you are not your behavior, and your behavior is not hopeless. New techniques have been discovered and developed to change how your brain is wired. And once you change your mental resources, your behavior will change automatically.

Step One Always Begins with Awareness

Many models of change begin and end with awareness. Awareness has been called everything from "mindfulness" to "boot strapping" to "keeping a stiff upper lip." Awareness is essential. But alone, it is an incomplete system. What matters is what you do with that awareness. Simply shining a light on something you don't like is seldom enough of a motivator to drive you to change your behavior.

My own mother only knew how to tell me what was "wrong" with me. She thought she was doing me a great favor by constantly reminding me of all the things about me that needed to be fixed. At five, she told me, "You're getting fat." She was always quick to point out how well her friends' children were doing, and how I should be more like them. I was bombarded with "awareness" about what I should be doing and how I should be doing it. But that never inspired me to change my behavior because in my mind, it was just more proof that I could not, that I was not capable. And, yes, that was my choice, my decision, based on beliefs I held to be true about myself.

What Is A Belief?

A belief requires two things. It must have *feeling* and it must have *proof*. Believing is not a conscious, intellectual process. Beliefs are installed in your subconscious mind only when you have strong feelings, positive or negative, coupled with some sort of proof. Your deepest beliefs, whatever they may be, run your life.

All Behavior Is Belief Driven

Belief drives both "good" behavior and "bad" behavior. I had a client who was so addicted to helping people that he would sometimes spend large amounts of money to help someone he didn't even like out of a bind. Together, we uncovered a memory from first grade where he noticed a girl with a severe handicap on the playground. No one was playing with her, so he spent the afternoon befriending her. When he returned home, he told his mother about it. She said, "Doesn't it feel good to make someone less fortunate feel good? You are a very good boy."

As young children, we have no filter. We simply accept and believe what we see, experience, and what people tell us. Brain science clearly defines this process. Dr. Bruce Lipton, cell biologist and bestselling author of *The Biology of Belief*, explains that a child's brain operates at Delta frequency (one-half to four cycles per second) from birth to about age two. And from two to six years old, the brain operates at Theta (four to eight cycles per second). Delta and Theta brain frequencies are the same neural state that hypnotherapists use to implant new behaviors into their clients. So, basically, children spend the first six years of life in a hypnotic trance recording all sensory experiences and learning complex motor programs for speech, crawling, standing, walking, running, jumping, eating, dressing and a host of other programs they will need to function as adults. Children learn massive amounts of information about the world and how it works with virtually zero ability to choose or reject the ideas that are presented to them. This lack of critical thinking means that whatever limiting or sabotaging beliefs they learn become their 'truth' and their subconscious mind will dutifully generate behaviors that are in alignment with their programmed truth.

Children are not capable of the kind of adult logical thought which occurs when the brain is operating at Beta frequency (thirteen to thirty cycles per second), which does not happen regularly until about the age of nineteen. (Blume, 1982)[4]

As adults, we act as if everything we learned in childhood was the absolute truth about how the world works. Hearing "You're a very good boy" was only a small part of the stimulus that created my client's behavior of extreme generosity. His mother also implanted in his young, receptive brain, "God will always take care of you and more good will come to you when you do good deeds." That belief, installed at a time when he *felt* deeply fulfilled, acknowledged, successful, and loved, combined with his *proof* that the little girl experienced happiness after receiving his attention, and his mother beamed with pride. All of those things combined helped to forge his lifelong habit of ever-escalating and downright extravagant giving and helping. No matter how much he gives, somehow, someway, more and more money flows into his life. The more he gives, the more he receives because that is what he believes to be true at a deep, unconscious level. His program works automatically and unconsciously.

This unconscious programming can work positively and negatively. Another client of mine was severely bullied in elementary school. This woman had a very difficult time making friends. During one of our sessions, we discovered that she had a deep seated belief that the world was not a safe or friendly place. No matter how hard she tried to make new friends, her bristly personality would drive away the nicest people and attract people who regularly hurt and disappointed her. That too, was just a pattern, or program, based on beliefs that were installed in her unconscious mind at an early age.

The good news is, beliefs can be changed. Scientists used to believe

---

4   Blume, WT: *Atlas of Pediatric Encephalography*, Raven Press, New York, 1982.

that most of what you learned between birth and about eight years old was permanently hardwired. You were stuck with it. If you had an unfortunate childhood with messed up parents, or a relative or caregiver who did more harm than good, you simply became "damaged goods," and there was nothing anyone could do. You just had to learn to live with it. However, recent discoveries about the brain's ability to dissolve old connections and grow new ones, challenges what was once thought impossible regarding change.

Our minds are almost completely programmed by the time we reach eighteen years old. We are born into this world a blank slate. We know absolutely nothing. We immediately begin to experience a world where we learn what the people around us know. And they can only teach us what they learned from the people they grew up with. That explains a few things, doesn't it?

According to Lissa Rankin, M.D. in her book *Mind Over Medicine*, a large percentage of the mental programs that will run our lives has been programmed into our unconscious mind by the time we are about six years old. She goes on to say that "Even if the unconscious mind of your adult self is filled with positive, hopeful thoughts, you operate from the subconscious mind 95 percent of the time."[5] And we wonder why we are thirty, fifty, or even eighty years old, still doing the same crazy behaviors.

But not all programs are bad. Walking, driving, tying your shoes are all helpful and even necessary programs.

What Is A Program And How Does It Help Me To Take Ownership?

Programs are a result of how the brain learns new things. The first time you do something new, it feels odd, awkward and not at all normal. That is because your unconscious mind has no reference for it. The behavior is completely new to your brain.

I remember teaching my niece how to tie her shoes. It's an easy thing to do, right? So why was my little niece having such a hard time with this easy task? She had no reference for that behavior. But after many repetitions and feeling confident about her new ability, the behavior

---

5 Rankin, Lissa. *Mind Over Medicine: Scientific Proof You Can Heal Yourself.* Carlsbad: Hay House, Inc., 2013, pages 30-31.

plus the emotion got loaded into her unconscious mind. Now she can tie her shoes so efficiently that she can do it without even looking, and while talking about something else entirely. The behavior called, 'shoe tying' has been programmed into her subconscious mind at such a deep level that it has become an unconscious, automatic behavior. This frees her conscious mind to do more important tasks, even while she ties her shoes.

You have internal, unconscious programs for literally thousands of behaviors. If you pay close attention to your mundane behaviors, you will begin to discover patterns that might even shock you. Do you always put your pants on right leg first? How about your shoes? Do you brush your hair and teeth the same way every morning? Do you eat with your fork in your right or left hand?

An American spy was captured during World War II because he unconsciously switched his fork from his left hand back to his right hand after cutting some meat. Germans cut and eat with the fork remaining in their left hand. Americans switch the fork back to their right hand to eat the bite of meat they just cut.

I tend to brush my teeth in exactly the same pattern every time. When I realized how much I behaved the same way every time, it freaked me out. I thought, wow, how boring and predictable I am! So I tried to consciously do things differently, just to see what happened. But that was far more boring! I found myself wasting a lot of time and effort on things that were better left to automatic programs.

Now I appreciate my helpful programs. They are my brain's way of helping me to traverse the day more efficiently. If I let my unconscious mind brush my teeth and even drive my car, I can use my conscious mind to focus more on where I am going and what I want to accomplish when I arrive. That is what makes us human.

Humans can connect their conscious mind to higher functions of creativity, compassion and joy by making the mundane unconscious and automatic. If you did not have this ability to store programs that help you accomplish everyday tasks, you would have to relearn every little task each time you wanted to do it. You would never accomplish anything and civilization would not exist.

When you know how programs work, you are empowered to not only embrace and be grateful for the ones that are helpful, but also to uncover the programs that seem to hurt or sabotage you. Appreciating those helpful programs will lead you to a deeper understanding of how your unwanted and destructive programs have been so persistent and difficult to change in the past. Once you learn the tools to change them, life will naturally become more manageable.

How To Re-Program Your Brain

From the point of view of your unconscious mind, there really are no "bad" programs. According to Dr. Mathew B. James, the Prime Directive of your unconscious mind is to preserve the body; basically, to keep you safe.[6] Let me say that again. Keeping you safe is the number one function of your unconscious mind. Underneath every single behavior, no matter how bad it appears to be, is a program that was "learned" at a time when you were either so young or so traumatized, you really were doing the best you could. Those programs got encoded into your unconscious mind with strong emotions, coupled with physical proof of their necessity. The only way to stop the behaviors they produce is to go in and clean up the underlying belief system.

That is why affirmations alone rarely work. If you have a very weak program, then yes, repeat positive statements to yourself. That may be all you need. But if you have developed a whopper of a program that is slowly killing you, you need to bring out the big guns, which I will tell you about in the next chapter.

Recent scientific discoveries have revealed that the brain *can* be changed. Literally. They call this new science Neuroplasticity. Scientists used to believe that the neural pathways in the brain that are created in early childhood were permanent and unchangeable. Scientists have now proven that old neural pathways can actually be physically dissolved and new ones can be created, with far less effort than anyone could have imagined.[7]

Brain science tells us that it takes four to seven days to create a new neural pathway, twenty-one days to create a new habit or behavior, and two to three years to hard wire it. My experience is even more dramatic than that.

---

[6] Accelerated NLP Practitioner Certification Training, Matthew B. James, Published by The Empowerment Partnership, version 8.0, August 2011.

[7] Rugnetta, Michael "Neuroplasticity" *Encyclopedia Britanica*, Encyclopedia Britanica, Inc., February 4, 2014 Web. (Accessed: March 8, 2014)

Instant Change, Using Nothing More Than My Imagination!

Because FasterEFT synthesizes the best of several different modalities, including EFT and NLP, I decided I wanted a deeper understanding of NLP. During my first certification in Neuro Linguistic Programming (NLP), I volunteered to be the demo for a process called "Mapping Across: Like to Dislike." The instructor asked for a volunteer who wanted to dislike something they currently loved. For me, that was coffee. I was drinking four to six large mugs of coffee a day. I could not climb out of bed without my coffee. Anyone who knew me would say, "Don't talk to her until she's had her coffee." Coffee was a big part of my social life, as well as my daily routine. I loved it, even though I knew it dehydrated my body and disrupted my energy level and moods. Plus, I just hate being controlled. I felt addicted to coffee. Every time I tried to quit, I suffered with severe withdrawal symptoms: migraine headaches, strong cravings, fatigue and even nausea. I felt very stuck, but also very motivated to rid myself of this behavior that I absolutely loved. So I raised my hand to volunteer.

Next, the instructor asked me if there was something similar, preferably a liquid, that I really hated. I did. I was at a natural health weekend seminar a few years before where I drank a shot glass of wheatgrass juice followed by a shot glass of very nasty tasting oil, all on an empty stomach. I was okay with the wheatgrass, but the oil pushed me over the edge. Within minutes, I made a run for it and threw up in the hotel lobby. A nasty taste, a physical pain in my tummy, the smell of vomit, plus the emotions of total embarrassment and disgust make a terrific "hated substance" mental resource. The instructor got very excited and shouted, "Perfect! Come on up!"

I stood on stage in front of 180 people as the instructor asked me to follow some easy instructions. I closed my eyes and imagined two mental 'pictures.' First, a happy coffee drinking picture, and second, my disgusting throwing up oil and wheatgrass picture. The only thing the instructor asked me to do was change the characteristics of the 'happy' picture to match the characteristics of the 'disgusting' picture. So, I made the happy picture darker, moved it down a little, added the sound of throwing up, the emotions I felt, and a few other things and then opened my eyes. I looked at the instructor and said, "I don't feel any different." Suddenly, the perfect cup of coffee appeared, and he shoved it up under my nose and asked, "You want some?" I involuntarily recoiled, like it was a snake. Tears started to well up in my eyes. I was totally and completely shocked. My mental program and belief that I was addicted to coffee had changed in a few minutes! At of the time of this writing, that was almost three years ago. I never had a single withdrawal symptom, and I still do not want to go near a cup of coffee.

How could that be? Did I rewire my brain by changing how I represented a past event in my mind? Could I have, in fact, physically re-directed a neural pathway? How else could I explain such an immediate and lasting change from nothing more than a simple mental exercise? And if it can happen with a coffee addiction, how about something more serious? This little demo raised more questions than it answered, and a door in my mind opened to infinite possibilities. All these years I have *believed* change had to be hard, if not impossible. Suddenly, I had a new *feeling* coupled with new *proof*. That is how you create a new belief!

I wish I could tell you that my entire life changed instantly in that moment, but that was just the beginning. I had to actually do the work of tapping on myself daily. You can turn a tiny speed boat around in a flash, but a giant oil tanker takes some time to turn around. *Or is that just another belief?* My coffee addiction was gone, but I still had a mountain of feelings and proofs about weight loss, depression, menopause, and several very real health issues I was facing, including an under active thyroid. I had spent decades building a mighty structure around these issues. When a mountain of negative ideas does battle with one little positive idea, guess which one is going to win? The one with the most resources! What I did have was a ray of hope, like a trickle of water that eventually has the power to carve the Grand Canyon. There was now a bright light at the end of a long, dark tunnel, beckoning me forward. And that is what I want this book to be for you.

Life Is A Process

Pain is inevitable, but suffering is optional. This book is a process. Know that each step along the way is part of that process. If you apply yourself at each step, you will find yourself basking in the bright light of a new life sooner than you ever thought possible. You cannot get it wrong. You process your life perfectly. Healing is not linear. There are hills and valleys, wide clear roads, and narrow lanes full of obstacles.

These twelve new steps invite you to notice where you are, love yourself anyway, and continue to move through the process.

Take ownership by noticing everything about your life. Take an inventory, and not just a negative one. Write down all of the good things you have ever experienced, with great detail and attention. Then, make a simple list of all the things in your life that you do not like and the things you would like to change. This is how to take real ownership of your life. When you are stuck in old programming, you often begin to act out as if you are the same age as when that program got installed. If you don't believe me, go to a family reunion and watch what happens. We all go right back to those old behaviors and perceptions because they are our unconscious mind's first and best reference about how to keep us safe.

For example, if you learned at two years old that the best way to control your environment and receive the attention you need to survive is to yell and throw a temper tantrum, and you continued to get away with that program, you may realize that you are still doing that at forty-five years old. Take ownership of the realization. Write it down, but try to avoid embellishing it with a big, ugly victim story. When you wallow in your old story of what happened, even if you are justified, it only serves to drop your energy down into a low vibration of guilt, blame, and shame. Just accept it. Write it down and know that your young unconscious mind learned a strategy, a coping mechanism, that has been working on your behalf to "keep you safe," even when it manifested the opposite of safety.

Throughout this book, you will gradually learn to make peace with your programs, so your unconscious mind can release them and create new, more effective programs that assist you in gaining what you really want out of life. You are not your programs. You are a magnificent spiritual being having a human experience with a physical human brain that is trying its best to help you.

Change is both an art and a science. There are many people out there who have created many different paths toward healing almost every problem that exists. The next chapter is about finding a path that works.

Begin to Take Ownership by doing the following exercises before moving on.

STEP ONE EXERCISES

Happy Journal
Buy a journal that you really love. Spend a few dollars and find one that makes you feel good when you look at it. Call this your Happy Journal. Begin by writing down twenty-five happy memories. Write down in detail what made you feel good — what you saw, heard, felt, smelled or tasted, and how good it made you feel at the time. The more detail, the better. People embellish their bad memories with magnificent detail. Give your good memories the same level of importance.

I have had clients in session who had difficulty searching for a single happy memory. If this is you, dig deep. It's not that you don't have any, you just have not spent much time focusing on them. Come up with as many as you can. Then go out and make some new ones. Don't wait for conditions to be perfect. Just do it and write them down in your Happy Journal. Most of us tend to invalidate our happy memories. Just because a relationship ended badly does not mean there were no happy moments along the way. Why do you focus on the bad stuff and completely forget about the good parts? Was the good stuff any less real? Who taught you that was the truth? Just notice. And add that to part two below.

Peace List
Buy a cheap spiral notebook and label it "Peace List." Don't bother writing a lot of detail or story. Simply make a bullet point list of everything you don't like in your life, and everything you would like to change. Do not dwell on it. If you find yourself getting sucked into the negativity, anger, sadness, resentment, guilt, judgment, depression, or anything else, take out your Happy Journal and read about some happy moments. Then, close your eyes and really feel the good feelings. Step into that happy memory. Be in your body and see what you saw, hear what you heard and feel what you felt that made you happy.

Continue this until it effectively overrides the bad feelings. It may take a few minutes because you are probably used to doing it the other way around. Stick with it. Take a deep breath and let all the good feelings settle into your body. Then come back to your Peace List later. Do not dwell on your Peace List or use it to beat yourself up. You will use it in later chapters to create deep and lasting change. One day soon, it may become your greatest gift.

Declare Who You Really Are

In every traditional Twelve Step Program, you are asked to state your name and then say "I am…" (Fill in your addiction). I'd like you to try something a little different. Stand and declare:

"My name is _____ and I am a magnificent child of God."

Or,

"My name is _____ and I am a magnificent Being."

Notice how that makes you feel. Journal about it. Keep saying it until you believe it.

STEP TWO

SEEK WISDOM AND APPLY IT

It may be that when we no longer know what to do, we have come to our real work, and when we no longer know which way to go, we have begun our real journey.

~Wendell Berry

For years, I was a self-help and seminar junkie. I bought every new book by every famous spiritual, motivational, and organizational author. I got very excited and turned on by each new insight, savoring the intellectual stimulation. But I never fully applied myself to any one thing in a deep and meaningful way. I was a dilettante. I studied one modality briefly, then I was on to the next. I never took the time to master anything. I knew a little about a lot of different things. I had cocktail knowledge—just enough to have an interesting conversation at a party.

Wisdom Without Action Is Empty And Useless
We are all seekers and doers. But most of us tend to get more excited about one than the other. The secret to having a joyful and fulfilled life is: *You have to do both.*

I bought more books than I had time to read. They still litter my office. I purchased them with the best of intentions, but I have yet to crack the covers of many of them. All that "shelf" help never translated to self-help. And then there were the seminars, both online and in person. My low sense of self-worth drove me to spend thousands of dollars on seminars that frankly would have been better spent on a vacation. I constantly sought answers from outside myself. I felt so broken. I searched long and hard for that one thing that could finally fix me.

Living my life from the recognition that I am not broken has been a massive change of perspective. I now realize that everything about me works perfectly, according to the life experiences that loaded automatic programs into my mind. I have been operating from ideas and unconscious programs that are inconsistent with what my adult conscious mind desires.

Action Without Wisdom Is Also Empty And Useless

Action without wisdom can waste time and be downright destructive. I have clients, friends, and family members who are all about action. They busy themselves working long hours, sacrificing relationships, and destroying their health trying to 'fix' everything. They tell themselves that hard work is a virtue and they settle for a badge of suffering, instead of working smarter and attaining the results they truly desire.

Which one are you? A seeker or a doer? Don't judge yourself for being one or the other. Simply notice if you recognize a pattern in your life. If you are really not sure, ask someone who knows you well and is willing and able to tell you in a kind way. As I said before, the secret is to do both. We will start with Seeking Wisdom.

Seek Wisdom

There are as many ways to do something as there are people doing it. Some are better than others. And of those that are better, one or two will really resonate with you personally. Seek wisdom that feels good to you.

Honor your intuition along the way. One of the most underdeveloped and undervalued skills in Western culture is the ability to utilize your intuition. Your intuition can manifest as an actual voice. But it is just as likely to come in the form of a gut feeling, sometimes subtle and sometimes wrenching. However it shows up for you, practice paying attention to and respecting your inner communication. You were probably never taught to listen to that still small voice within. Maybe you were told your inner voice was "impractical dreaming" or even "the voice of the devil." If so, you may have inadvertently tuned out the source of all your power and creativity. Your power and creativity speaks to you from inside.

That said; do not believe everything your mind tells you. That inner vision, voice, or feeling is your connection to both your Higher Power and your subconscious mind. The challenge is to distinguish between the two. The best way to recognize your truth is to notice if the communication comes from pain or joy. Negative mental programs emerge from pain and eventually cause more pain. Your Higher Power, however you define it, is the source and substance of all joy.

EFT and FasterEFT

I began my tapping journey with traditional EFT, founded by Gary Craig. EFT (the Emotional Freedom Technique) is a system of gently tapping acupressure points on the body while talking about and feeling negative emotions. EFT teaches that the Chinese meridian system carries impulses from the brain to the body, operating under the assumption that these pathways can become blocked or clogged. EFT assumes that the tapping unblocks those pathways.

FasterEFT operates under a different assumption: that the meridian system carries messages from the brain to the body, and those signals are directed by your thoughts. FasterEFT teaches that tapping interrupts the fear-based message from the brain to the body. This provides an immediate calming relief to the body, giving the brain an opportunity to learn new ways of dealing with the problem it is experiencing. FasterEFT does not teach that the meridian system can get blocked. Rather, that the system works perfectly all the time, based on the beliefs you hold to be true.

FasterEFT works so well because it utilizes your existing mind/body system. It teaches you how to identify negative mental programs and change them, using the same mental system which created them.

For example, let's say you are walking down a dark alley. Someone jumps out, points a gun at you, and says "Give me your wallet." (In pre-historic times, the threat might have been a saber toothed tiger instead of a mugger, but the brain/body mechanism still operates the same way.)

Upon seeing the mugger, your brain would sense danger, according to your internal references, and it would signal your heart to beat faster and your lungs to breathe in more air. Your blood pressure would go up, and all the energy would leave your core and go out to your arms and legs, preparing you to either fight, freeze, or run. Digestion would shut down, and your blood would be redirected to your vital organs, away from the brain, thereby diminishing logic and reason. Your liver, kidneys, adrenals, and many other organs would shut down normal activities and switch to producing hundreds of chemicals to aid in your fight-or-flight response. And that's just for starters!

Your mind and body are hard wired to keep you safe, and the lengths it will go to are immense. The mind cannot distinguish between something that is happening in the moment and something that happened thirty years ago. If you have a traumatic event in your past and you close your eyes and recreate it in your mind — imagine that mugger, bully, or abuser — your body can receive the same exact signal from the brain and move into that full blown fight-or-flight response as if you were back there now.

When you relive your past traumas every day, imagining them in great detail, complete with color, sound, smell, taste, feeling, and emotion, that wreaks havoc on your physical and mental health. That is what happens inside the mind of a person with PTSD (Post Traumatic Stress Disorder). They are stuck in a loop, replaying traumatic memories. Their bodies do not know they are no longer in danger. They continue to live in the state of terror and stress that originated with the traumatic event.

PTSD is not just for soldiers and victims of war. Many of the FasterEFT clients who come to me for help have experienced horrific childhood abuse and are stuck with traumatic memories that plague them every day. Those experiences (emotions plus proofs) create powerful belief systems that drive all kinds of behaviors, including addictions. You don't need to actively think about the past trauma for it to affect your well-being and your behavior. The trauma, once loaded into your subconscious mind, creates a belief system, and those subconscious beliefs drive behavior automatically, even when you are unaware of their existence.

A belief that the world is a scary place filled with people who want to hurt you can create anything from a heroin addict trying to escape their mental torment by using drugs, to an extremely successful person who uses money to build a financial wall of protection. How an individual decides to process a trauma and what options they believe they can create to escape the pain, affects their outcome.

What Do I Do With My Negative Emotions?

FasterEFT offers a fast and easy way to release the pain out of your memories so you can be free of the mental torture that drives what we label "bad behavior." That is why I tell my clients, "You are *not* your behavior."

My issue with the traditional twelve step program is the requirement of labeling people as broken, diseased, and without hope of ever being free of that label. I do not believe it helps to claim a personal identity associated with your problem. That seems like the opposite of healing. What you put after the words "I am ... " tends to become a self-fulfilling prophecy. You are *not* your behavior. You act in a certain way because your unconscious mind has learned a skill that it believes helps you, even if it is actually killing you. And your mind will continue to do that behavior out of love and perceived protection until you teach your unconscious mind to change its perception of your past. Doing so will immediately change your present and dramatically transform your future.

You are not your behavior. You are a magnificent human being with interesting skills and coping mechanisms that can be released and transformed with a little effort and skilled guidance. The problem is not the alcohol, drug, food, porn, shopping, or gambling. Those are merely the coping mechanisms of choice.

Sitting around replaying horror stories reinforces fear based behaviors. Retelling stories makes them bigger, instead of ridding yourself of them. Even if you understand your trauma from every angle, that trauma will remain with you, unless you do something different. Buried emotions never die. They continue to reappear in different and often uglier ways. If you want to change your behavior, you must alter your subconscious mind by cleaning up your past. Only then can you begin to create new patterns of being that lead to a better and happier life. FasterEFT is a great tool to help you achieve deep and lasting change.

What Is FasterEFT?

The creator and founder of FasterEFT, Robert G. Smith, combined traditional EFT tapping with concepts from several other modalities, especially NLP (Neuro Linguistic Programming). NLP is the study of how the mind and body work as one system, not two. Robert Smith streamlined the insights and procedures of NLP, making them faster and easier. FasterEFT addresses the mind/body connection in a way that gives you control of your thoughts and emotions. It speaks directly to the subconscious mind, enabling the body to reduce stress and relieve physical and emotional symptoms.

FasterEFT empowers you to change how you internally represent your past, which then opens you to accept new possibilities for your present and your future. This naturally creates a positive effect in the quality of your life. This universal healing tool addresses virtually anything, including but not limited to: addictions, allergies, anxiety, bad habits, cravings, creative blocks, depression, dis-ease, fatigue, fears, grief and loss, headaches, insomnia, low self-esteem, phobias, body image, and weight. As you change what you hold within, your body and your world will automatically begin to express your new belief.

How Does Tapping Work?

Tapping works with the Chinese meridian system, which is the same system used in acupuncture. The main difference being, you tap on the points instead of sticking needles into them. When a stressful situation occurs, the organs in your body respond with all the reactions and body chemistry they can muster to either fight off or outrun your problem. The fight-or-flight response is your body's best response to what your brain deems a stressful situation.

The memory of the distress encodes itself into your neurology using your body's response. FasterEFT has you tap on the acupressure points that correspond to the primary organs associated with the fight or flight response. The tapping interrupts the distress message from the brain to the body. That allows the body to relax and release the negative emotions out of the memory. FasterEFT works simply and elegantly.

Apply Wisdom

Research has shown that the most successful people are those who do one thing and do it incredibly well. In his book *Flow*, Mihaly Csikszentmihalyi claims that greatness requires an enormous commitment of time—about 10,000 hours. From the Beatles to Bill Gates, anyone who has achieved great success has invested a lot of time to become an expert. Ten thousand hours is an enormous commitment. The only way a sane person could apply themselves to one thing for that many hours and still be happy, would be because they absolutely loved what they were doing.

I once knew a musician who practiced so late into the night that he would fall asleep cradling his guitar. When he woke up the next morning, he strummed a tune before getting out of bed. Instead of seeing his practice as a painful duty, he saw it as an act of love, not a means to rack up his 10,000 hours toward expertise.

An amazing couple, Kip and Mona Lisa Harding, are homeschooling their ten children, the six oldest of which all started college by the age of twelve. What is their secret? Not genius IQs, according to the Hardings. They simply allow their children to pursue their passions. Mona Lisa says, "By finding out what they really like to study and allowing them to go deep into one subject, they learned more quickly, got less bored, and naturally excelled." Kip says, "The expectation is that you're going to have a fun day, not that you're going to come home with A's. They're normal kids. They just don't wait till they're older to figure out what they love in life."

If you have children, you may want to check out their tips for raising a happy and successful family at www.collegeby12.com. When you love what you do, it's not hard and it's not work.

Finding a technique that really lights you up, turns you on, and actually *works*, motivates you to set aside everything else and allow yourself to go deep with that one thing. Tapping remains the easiest and fastest method I have ever encountered to create deep and lasting change.

The reason I searched endlessly for something that would "fix" my problems was because most of what I tried either failed to work or did not hold my interest. FasterEFT worked quickly and at a deep level the very first time I tried it. It's hard to argue with profound results.

How To Tap

Tapping FasterEFT style is very simple. There are two major components: Aim and Fire. The way you aim at your problem is to think about it. Actually close your eyes and imagine your problem. Step into the memory and see what you saw, feel what you felt, and hear what you heard. Notice how strong the negative emotions and feelings are. Rate them from zero to ten with ten representing the strongest feelings you can imagine. The more associated you are with the feeling, the faster you can let go of the negative emotion. Then, use your first two fingers to gently tap on acupressure points on the body while saying, "Let it go." Take your mind off the problem while you tap. Focus on the feel of your fingers tapping on your skin as you tell your unconscious mind, "Let it go."

Earlier tapping protocols (TFT and EFT) were far more complicated and required you to tap on many more points, while you continued to talk about the problem. FasterEFT focuses on five points along the meridian system:

- Between the Eyes

- Side of the Eye

- Under the Eye

- On the Collar Bone

- Around Your Wrist (which activates the many points in your hand.)

Tap three to seven times on each point as you say out loud, "Let it go. It's okay to let it go. It's safe to let it go. I'm letting it go now." After tapping, squeeze your wrist, take a deep breath in, blow it all away, and say the word "Peace."

Now, take a quick break and go to a happy memory. This pulls you completely out of the old negative program. Step into the happy memory as if you were there. Feel all the good feelings that you felt back then and enjoy them.

Then go back and check the bad feeling. If it's still there, notice how it has changed. Zero to ten, how big is it now? Tap another round.

Repeat this process until the negative feelings are completely gone. Persistence is your friend.

Watch a basic "How To Tap" video here: www.FasterEFTworks.com/videos.

See the Appendix at the end of this book for more links to "follow along" online tapping videos.

STEP TWO EXERCISES

Practice Tapping
Choose a problem. Start with a minor one.

- Close your eyes and imagine your problem. Step into the memory and see what you saw, feel what you felt, and hear what you heard.

- Notice how strong the negative emotions and feelings are. Rate them from zero to ten with ten representing the strongest feelings you can imagine.

- Use your first two fingers to gently tap. Take your mind off the problem while you tap. Focus on the feel of your fingers tapping on your skin.

- Tap between your eyes and say "Let it go."

- Tap the side of your eye and say "It's safe to let it go."

- Tap under your eye and say "It's okay to let it go."

- Tap on your collar bone and say "I'm letting it all go now."

- Grab your wrist and give it a squeeze. Take a deep breath in. Blow it out and say "Peace."

- Recall a happy memory and enjoy it. If needed, use your Happy Journal. Step into your happy memory. See, hear, feel, and experience everything that made it good.

- Go back and check the problem and notice how it feels now.

- Repeat the process. Keep tapping on every aspect of the memory until you change the meaning of it. Turn it into a positive so it no longer bothers you.

Dedicate yourself to tapping. Tap DAILY! You will love the results as you become the expert regarding your own emotional intelligence.

STEP THREE

DEVELOP INNER COMMUNICATION SKILLS

If you fail to control your own mind, you may be sure you will control nothing else.

~Napoleon Hill

I recently attended a workshop on how to communicate more effectively with other people. I also have numerous books and audio programs about how to be an effective public speaker. But I rarely hear about seminars that teach ways to improve how I communicate with myself. Learning how to talk to myself almost sounds silly. People who walk around talking to themselves are usually labeled crazy, right?

But think about it. Who is the number one most important relationship in your life? Who do you spend the most time with? Wherever you go and whatever you do, who is there? *You.* Are you even aware of the kind of relationship you have with yourself?

What Does Your Inner Dialogue Sound Like?
Are you nice to yourself? Or are you hard on yourself? The way you learned to talk to yourself comes directly from the people you were exposed to as a child. Their words and repeated phrases implanted themselves deep in your unconscious mind before you had filters or any idea that you could object. The words and phrases spoken by your

care givers, siblings, teachers, ministers, and friends eventually became the recordings that now rule your mind and run your emotions.

In reality, there is only one thing in life that you have absolute control over and that is your thoughts. No person or thing can control your thoughts unless you allow it. Maybe you were taught that you had no right to think an original thought. Know that you did the best you could under difficult circumstances. You acquired and practiced patterns of thought that served you back when you were a child. They helped you survive. But if those thoughts are not serving you now, you have the ability to change them. And you are the only person with the power to change them. A FasterEFT practitioner can guide you through the process, but ultimately, you are the only one controlling your inner thoughts. So why do you feel like your thoughts are controlling you?

As a child, were you ever told to sit down and be quiet? Were you ever punished for blurting out your authentic truth? In school, were you encouraged to speak your mind and solve problems your own way? Or did your teachers expect you to do things their way? At work, were you ever promoted for pointing out old, inefficient practices and suggesting better methods? Or did your boss support only those who were on board with their agenda? You have had a lifetime of squashing your inner voice and personal truth. Sometimes that truth is buried so deep, it takes practice just to find it.

The Power of Your Thoughts

Your thoughts are the building blocks of your power. Everything that has ever existed began as a thought. This book began as a thought. The chair you are sitting on began as a thought in someone's mind. Buildings, cars, pencils, toilets, cigarettes and weddings all began as a thought. So did war and genocide. Every single thing you can think of began as a thought in someone's mind. You have the power and free will to create absolutely anything. And you do, all the time.

Every day I hear people say, "I can't create what I want because ... " and then they offer an excuse. Actually, they are always creating what they want. Or more precisely, their unconscious mind is creating what it wants and needs to feel safe.

The FasterEFT belief system suggests that something inside your unconscious mind has created what you have now to fulfill a deeply rooted intention that you may not even be aware of. Your unconscious intentions often contradict everything you say you want. Your life right now is a perfect creation, the result of beliefs that are alive and locked inside your unconscious mind. Believe it or not, you are committed to having exactly what you have right now, even if it is because you don't believe you could have something better. That may sound harsh, but it's true. If you were committed to something different, you would have that.

I am not telling you this so you can beat yourself up. I want you to increase your awareness and loving self-acceptance. Once you know and accept exactly where you are, you can plan your journey to a new destination. FasterEFT can help you take control of your thoughts so you can take charge of your life. That is real personal power.

Thoughts Become Things

In my late thirties, I grew very tired of being a single lady. I longed for a loving, fun and compatible relationship. So, one day, in a very emotional moment, I sat down and wrote a list of qualities I desired in a mate along with a list of qualities I would bring to the relationship. My list was not a request. It was a vision and a declaration accompanied by intense emotion. When I was done writing and a bit calmer, I folded my piece of paper and put it in a drawer where I completely forgot about it. Less than two months later, I had a blind date with a man who matched almost every item on my list. We married about a year later.

Most people will tell you that action creates things. And it does. I had to actually go on that blind date, something I had sworn I would never do again. But what creates action? Belief drives the kind of action you choose to take and thoughts create the belief.

I have created many seemingly improbable things and situations through persistent thought, which created a belief that caused me to take certain actions. Some were beneficial, like a car I desired. Even though it was out of my price range, I found a pre-owned one I could afford. Some of my persistent thoughts have caused problems. Too much worry has actually made me sick. Luckily, not every thought I have had manifested immediately.

We have all had the occasional nasty thought, wishing someone were dead or hurt or sent away. Those kinds of thoughts usually come in response to the perception, "They are hurting me." Fortunately, the majority of us never act out those fleeting thoughts. The continual, persistent and repeated thoughts that dominate our consciousness are the ones that become real manifested objects, events, and behaviors. It is the atmosphere of our thoughts that affects our life in real and chronic ways. When we look at thoughts in terms of trends, rather than individual things, then we can see just how real they are.

Affirmations Alone Do not Work

If thoughts become things, that means thoughts are creative. They become real according to the degree of emotion and conviction behind them. If you weigh three hundred and fifty pounds and you start repeating the thought, "I am skinny, I am skinny," over and over inside your head, that new thought will most likely encounter a barrage of emotionally charged contradictory thoughts creating a 'positive versus negative' thought battle. Anyone who has tried to change their brain using affirmations alone knows what I'm talking about. The thought with the most resources always wins.

Everything you say and think is an affirmation. Unfortunately, much of what we say and think is negative. If you want to use positive affirmations, make sure you create ones that make you feel strong positive emotions. Emotions contain the fuel you need to drive the behavior you want. The affirmations with the strongest emotions and the most proof are the ones that stick and become your reality.

So How Do I Change The Big Ones?

When your biggest negative, fearful thoughts and memories have been running your mind and body for a long time, you may feel like it's impossible to change them. You can spend years in therapy trying to understand why the terrible things you wrote down on your Peace List happened to you. Unfortunately, *why* is not the most productive question to ask. Sometimes, bad things just happen. You were in the wrong place at the wrong time. Your power lies in how you respond to those events and in the meaning you give to them. You can have all the understanding in the world and still have your problem.

The key to change is altering the emotional charge on your thoughts. Making peace with your past is the fastest and easiest way to transform the thoughts and beliefs that dominate your mind. Once you create a new set of dominant thoughts, your whole life changes. What you think about and believe creates more of the same.

Ready To Change Some Thoughts?

Changing the thoughts that have been causing you pain and problems ranks among the most important actions you can take to heal your life. But how do you do that? You cannot successfully plan a trip without first knowing where you are. Try buying a trip to Paris online without first entering your departure city. You won't receive any results because you cannot plan a journey without first knowing your starting point. Let's do an exercise to discover the exact nature of your current inner dialogue.

This exercise will assist you in uncovering valuable information about what programs are buried deep in your subconscious mind. Your mental programs generally operate in the background without you even knowing they are there. But when you challenge them, they tend to pop up, usually with words, feelings, memories, or sensations. Write them down. Once you know the mental programs you are dealing with, you can make a plan to change them. On the other hand, if you identify a positive, helpful belief, amplify it. Enjoy it. Then write that great belief and how good it makes you feel in your Happy Journal.

Grab a pen and paper and find a comfortable place where you will not be disturbed. Use the statements below as writing prompts. Close your eyes and repeat the first statement to yourself several times. Notice what comes up. How do you respond to the statement? Does it make you feel angry? Uncomfortable? Do you hear a snappy comeback like "Yeah, right!" Perhaps you hear the voice of a parent or teacher telling you what they think. You may even have a progression of responses. Your initial reaction may be anger that later turns into sadness. Whatever you experience, write it all down. Spend enough time on each statement to notice the emotions each phrase triggers in you. Your subconscious mind may let you avoid buried beliefs for a short while, but if you repeat the statement long enough, any unconscious objections will eventually surface. Don't analyze what comes up. Just notice it and write it down. Take a few minutes now to discover the content of your inner dialogue.

Repeat each statement to yourself, then write down what emotions come up for you:

- I am gorgeous

- I am powerful

- I am lovable

- I am stupid

- I am a genius

- Change is easy

- I deserve to be happy

- I deserve to be a success

- There is something wrong with me

- I forgive them

- I forgive myself

- I love myself

- I deserve to live

Here's what happened the first time I practiced this exercise. I said to myself "I am perfect." I first had a warm feeling that yes, spiritually speaking, I am perfect. So I said it a few more times inside my head. What eventually came up was, "Yeah, right." Then I heard, "You are perfect except for all that fat. And those arms. And that neck!" Suddenly, a long list of what was "wrong" with me started pouring into my head. Every time I said "I am perfect," I felt that it was not true, followed by a list of proofs. My inner voice reminded me of my mother's voice when I was growing up. She was very good at pointing out what was wrong and rarely did she mention any positive qualities about me.

My inner dialogue was critical, negative, and invalidating. Essentially, not very nice. The voice was neither angry nor loud, just matter of fact and harshly judgmental, just like Mama. As a result, I had a hard time achieving anything in my life because as soon as I started, I would criticize myself until I decided it was just not worth trying anymore. I was the perpetual starter who never finished anything. Finishing this book has been my very own tapping miracle!

What did you learn about the tone of *your* inner dialogue? Was it primarily negative or positive? Was the dialogue dismissive and hurtful or encouraging and supportive? Do you mentally beat yourself up or do you treat yourself like a good friend? If you are struggling with negative self-talk like I was, you are not alone.

People who are kind to themselves are having a happy, fulfilled life. Now, you are going to learn how you can too. Use your list of emotional responses to make some positive changes to your inner dialogue. If you have not done the above exercise, do it now and then come back to this next section.

Tap It Down; Tap It Up Technique

Awareness is always the first step to change. What you do with your awareness makes all the difference. Since you learned how to tap in the last chapter, you are now going to apply the tapping technique to your list of negative words, phrases, feelings, and memories. Take each negative word or phrase you wrote down, one at a time, and do this FasterEFT technique:

Notice the bad feeling that goes with the words that came up for you. Remember how it felt. Close your eyes and really go there. If it was a memory, see what you saw, hear what you heard, and feel what you felt. Say those words you do not like out loud and ask yourself, "From zero percent to one hundred percent, how true is that negative feeling and statement right now?" Notice the number. Feel it for the last time. Imagine a tree for a moment. If someone pulled all the roots out from under that tree, what naturally happens to a tree without roots? That's right, it falls over and dies. Now, tap and say these phrases out loud:

- Tap *between your eyes* and say: "I release and let it go."

- Tap the *side of your eye* and say: "Whatever this means, I'm letting it go."

- Tap *under your eye* and say: "I release and let it go now."

- Tap on your *collar bone* and say: "It's safe to let it all go now."

- Squeeze your *wrist* and say: "I'm letting it go and I'm ok."

- Take a deep breath in, then blow it all away, and say, "Peace."

- Go to a happy memory and enjoy how good that feels for a minute.

- Then, go back and check the feeling that used to be bad.

- Notice if the feeling is still there or if it is gone. If it is still there, notice what is left. From zero to one hundred percent how true is it now?

Tap over and over again, as many rounds as needed, until the emotion is down to zero. When the statement is no longer true for you, then state the opposite. For example, if the statement was, "I am stupid," then say, "I am smart." Use your intuition and allow your unconscious mind to give you the positive statement you want to tap up.

Ask yourself, from zero to one hundred percent, how true is that positive statement right now? If the positive statement is anything less than one hundred percent, then notice the part that is not true yet and tap it away. Say your positive statement again and keep tapping until it is one hundred percent true!

Then go to another negative response and tap it down. Then tap up its opposite positive statement and good feeling.

Repeat this process for each negative statement or feeling that you wrote down during the previous exercise. If you cannot complete the exercise now, set aside a period of time when you can tap uninterrupted. It may take hours or even a few sessions over several days. But it is well worth your time. Clearing your negative self-talk improves your inner dialogue. Changing your inner dialogue alters your entire life.

Continue to develop your FasterEFT tapping skills. Spend time every day studying and practicing. Your whole life will change. There are hundreds of resources online for FasterEFT. Robert Smith has almost a thousand free videos, including dozens of amazing testimonials, online at www.YouTube.com/HealingMagic.

If you have a problem that feels daunting to deal with on your own, visit www.FasterEFT.com/Practitioners to find a practitioner in your area or one you would feel comfortable working with over Skype or Facetime.

When To Tap
The secret to fast and easy change is to tap in the moment. As soon as you feel something come up—a craving, an anger, a frustration, a disappointment, or a jerk who cut you off in traffic, tap immediately in the heat of the moment. Tap on every unproductive or hurtful thought. Stop and tap until you are free from the tyranny and torture of those old thoughts and emotions. Don't wait until you cool off. Tap while those thoughts and emotions are lit up inside you. The stronger those negative feelings are, the faster you will eliminate them. If you wait until later, the feelings will be weaker and more elusive. Strong feelings are evidence of resistance.

Resistance Is Your Friend
What you resist, persists! To resist something means you choose to avoid it because you think it will be difficult or unpleasant. You don't want to go there, so you resist it.

In electrical terms, a resistor is something that reduces the electrical current and dissipates the energy. When you resist doing something that can benefit you, you restrict and dissipate the flow of your good. When air, water, or energy stop flowing, they stagnate and breed nasty things. Being stuck means you are resisting something. What are you resisting? What are you avoiding?

There are two sides to every issue. The unproductive, unhappy side usually involves resistance while the happy and productive side is a sign of unrestricted flow. For instance, are you embracing health, or resisting illness? Are you embracing wealth, or resisting poverty. Are you actively loving your partner, or are you resisting any possibility of heartbreak? When you resist something you don't want, you block the flow of your good and create more of what you don't want. When you are joyfully focused on what you do want and the creative process, you step into the flow of your good.

You are always thinking and doing something. The trick is to become aware of what that is. Notice if those thoughts and behaviors are benefiting you and making you happy or if they are hurting you and making you miserable. If you are miserable, that is a symptom of resistance.

Resistance comes in many forms. To give an example, do you wake up thinking "I am the luckiest person alive to have a job that I love that pays me so much money?" Or are you awake half the night thinking

"How am I going to pay my rent this month? I hate that I never have enough money and I have to spend all my time working for jerks."

If you believe that changing your life requires you to spend time resisting and fighting all your old negative beliefs, then you will have a life of resisting and fighting. When you truly let go of an old belief, your identity changes. The old thoughts are no longer inside you because they are simply not who you are anymore. If you feel old negative thought patterns creeping back in, that means you have not let go of all aspects of the old belief. There are some stragglers. The part you let go of is gone. But there are many aspects and roads to our subconscious beliefs. Go in and clean up all the remaining parts and pieces. Then you will enjoy your new positive beliefs unencumbered because the old ones will be completely gone.

Many traditional forms of help, like the traditional twelve step program, advocate that you can never be rid of your old thought programs completely, suggesting that you must learn how to live with your pain. Resist it as hard as you can, one day at a time. In that model, your problem defines you and locks you into a permanent and unchangeable identity. FasterEFT teaches that no matter how bad your problem is, you *can* let it all go and be free to change and adopt a new identity. That idea is substantiated by the new discoveries in brain science regarding neuroplasticity.

Knowing that all behavior is the result of unconscious belief, you can use resistance as your guide. Whenever you notice yourself resisting something, your unconscious mind is showing you a hidden belief that drives behaviors and feelings. Resistance is a great opportunity. Use it. Tap it away. The only way to experience true free will is to clear away all resistance. Then will you operate from real choice and personal preference, instead of from unconscious programs created when you were a child. Resistance is your friend in transformation. Pay attention to it and apply your skills to it.

Results Don't Lie

Results are my score card. As much as I sometimes hate admitting it, my results show me how I am doing with my thoughts. It's easy to blame circumstances or other people for my problems. There may even be some circumstances where I would be absolutely justified in blaming someone else. But then I look at someone like Nick Vujicic.

Nick is about three feet tall. He was born without arms or legs. If anyone has an excuse for not being a success in life, he does. Yet, he is a powerful and successful public speaker and an inspiration to millions of people. Nick often delivers his speeches perched on a long table on stage. He moves energetically back and forth across the table, speaking from his heart. He has a tiny appendage of a foot he calls "my little chicken wing," which he uses to kick a phone up in the air and catch with his shoulder and chin. He brings his entire audience through laughter and tears to profound inspiration. And at the end of every speech, he invites the entire audience to come up and give him a hug. Hundreds of people line up to hug him one by one as they leave his presentation. Try watching one of his speeches on YouTube.

How does someone with that level of disability create a successful life? What type of inner communication skills must he have to wake up every morning and decide to have a great day? If Nick can dream up a life he'd like to live and then go out and do it, so can you and I. Check out Nick Vujicic at www.AttitudeIsAltitude.com.

What do we all have in common with someone like Nick? We have a mind and the power to think. When you stop giving your power away to circumstances and work at mastering your thoughts, then you embrace your true power.

Accept Your Power

In Western culture, we have been taught to believe that our greatest power lies in having and doing. We believe that we must *have* something, like money, so we can *do* something, like buy a new car, so we can *be* something, like happy or respected. But the most successful people in the world know that it begins with how we are *being*.

When you are being powerful, happy, or peaceful, how you are being drives your actions, and you naturally do things that allow you to have what you really want. Having what you desire begins inside your mind.

Give yourself the gift of practicing FasterEFT and develop a mindset of personal power. Release the old, false beliefs in your powerlessness and helplessness. Let go of the victimhood and step into response-ability. Respond in new ways to circumstances and you will create new circumstances that match your new perspective. Step into your power. Tap into your power!

STEP THREE EXERCISES

Take Control of Your Inner Dialogue
If you have not done the exercise earlier in this chapter, go back and do it now.

- Pay attention to your inner dialogue and tap away the thoughts and feelings you don't like.

- Don't believe everything you think. If your brain is telling you something you don't like or do not agree with, tell it to "Shut up!" Then tell yourself the truth, in a loving way. This will take practice. But it is a great skill to develop.

- Tap to release those negative thought bombs.

Peace List
Use these guidelines to add to your Peace List:

Include every circumstance or person you need to make peace with in your life. Add every bad situation you have experienced, witnessed or were told about that had a negative emotion, even if it doesn't bother you now. You don't need to write the story, just list your age, a title for each memory, plus the emotions you felt during the experience. Example: Age six, Teacher taped my mouth shut. Fear, shame, guilt, violated. Note the emotions you felt back then and now.

Note: If you get stuck in a negative emotional state while working on your Peace List, put it away and go read your Happy Journal. You can also tap to let it go.

- Birth: list any situations or stories you were told.

- Relationships with siblings and family members, how you felt about them and how they treated you.

- Any sexual abuse.

- Your first sexual experience, particularly negative emotions. (If sex was great, put it in your Happy Journal!)

- Emotional or physical abuse or traumas.

- School experiences, issues with teachers, classmates, etc.

- Major moves, changing schools.

- Deaths of pets, pet injuries, losses.

- Any romantic relationship hurts, especially first boyfriend or girlfriend.

- Pivotal points in life with parents, siblings, bosses, co-workers, and others.

- Divorce, relationship breakups, broken friendships.

- Deaths, grief and loss, loss of job, loss of health.

- All hurts, anything you felt bad about when it happened.

- All major medical illnesses, chronic illnesses, other medical problems.

- Accidents and injuries.

- Fears and phobias with experiences that support them.

Happy Journal

Continue to add fun, joyful memories to your Happy Journal. Ask friends and family to remind you of fun times. Start creating new happy memories and write them down immediately. Read your Happy Journal whenever you want to feel better.

STEP FOUR

RECOGNIZE THE POWER OF THE MIND/BODY CONNECTION

Anyone who does not believe in the Mind Body Connection has obviously never had a sexual fantasy.

~Louise Hay

Imagine a big, juicy lemon. Now imagine cutting it in half, and then quarters. See the juice squirting onto your hands. Imagine smelling that strong lemon smell as you pick up one of the lemon wedges and bring it to your mouth. As the juice drips all the way down your arm, imagine taking a big bite into that juicy lemon. The tart tangy juice pops and squirts into your mouth and strikes the inside of your cheeks ...

What's happening inside your mouth? Are you puckering? Was there a change in the amount of saliva you were producing? About ninety percent of the people who read about the lemon don't even have to close their eyes to have a real body reaction. Their mind easily accepts the suggestion of a tart, juicy lemon, and their body produces a real physical reaction, based on their past references.

My husband, Dovell, loves to tell a story about a prank he pulled in high school. The school choir had rehearsed long and hard for an upcoming concert. They wanted to practice in front of a live audience, so they invited their friends to watch. My husband and three of his buddies parked themselves in the front row and waited patiently for the song that had a difficult whistling section. Just as the whistling started, they all pulled out big wedges of lemon and started to eat them. They slurped the lemons and puckered their lips. Their friends in the choir caught sight of this and suddenly, no one could whistle. Dovell and his cohorts were ordered to leave the rehearsal hall. They protested, declaring that they were not doing anything to anyone. They were merely snacking on lemons. But the teacher recognized the power of suggestion and threw them out.

Where the Mind Goes, the Body Follows

If you had a physical reaction to my description of biting a lemon, how did that happen? There are no lemons in this book. It happened because of a basic principle: Where the mind goes, the body follows. Your mind tends to go where it has already been. If you have never tasted a raw lemon before, you probably had no reaction. But if you have bitten into a lemon in the past and had a strong reaction, then you were more likely to have had a strong reaction to my lemony suggestion.

One System, Not Two

Most people refer to the mind and body as if they were two separate systems. The mind and body are actually two aspects of one system. We cannot separate mind from body or body from mind without destroying the whole system. We are human beings. *Human* refers to the body aspect and *being* refers to the mind/spirit aspect. Together, they comprise one whole system.

When we see ourselves from the perspective of wholeness, everything changes. Most of us are so busy trying to manage our physical bodies, other people, and our environment that we don't make time to manage our internal, mental, and emotional lives. Physical challenges can become so urgent that we often prioritize them over mental and emotional issues. It appears logical to occupy our time with the physical, tangible problems around us, including the destructive behaviors we refer to as addictions.

I dislike the word *addiction* because it implies that the behavior is caused only by the substance. FasterEFT operates from the belief that all behavior is the expression of conscious or unconscious belief, including addiction. The addiction to the substance or behavior is a symptom of a deeper problem. After clearing the deeper problem, the need for the substance can then be eliminated. And it sometimes disappears on its own.

I worked with a male client at a drug rehabilitation center in Hawaii who had an addiction to methamphetamine, which he administered intravenously. During a two hour FasterEFT crossfire session, he let go of several of his biggest childhood traumas. After we removed the primary emotional drivers that originally sent him to drugs for emotional relief, he was able to completely release his attachment to the physical behavior of loading a syringe and shooting up meth. After just one two hour session, he no longer wanted anything to do with his previous addiction. So, was he really addicted to meth? Or was something else happening? Watch his before and after interview video here: www.youtube.com/watch?v=Czg7puyp1Mg.

All behavior is driven by belief. Once you understand belief as strong emotions based on meaning you gave to a personal experience, then you have the key to changing behavior. FasterEFT teaches that working only on your behavior fails because behaviors are merely effects. Why spend years working and struggling to create change at the level of behavior when all it does is defeat and demoralize you? Even if you do manage to control a behavior, if that behavior was serving a strong mental purpose, your subconscious mind will either recreate it or find a different behavior to take its place.

Many twelve step meetings offer caffeinated beverages, sugary snacks, and a place to smoke cigarettes, reasoning that those substances are better than drugs and alcohol. When the underlying cause still exists, relapse looms heavily. Buried emotions never die. They fester beneath the surface of consciousness until they eventually erupt in old and new behaviors.

Refocusing your efforts onto transforming the life experiences and negative emotions that underlie behavior succeeds because those experiences and emotions are the true cause and driver of addiction. Until you go inside your mind, find the underlying cause, and pull it out by the roots, the behavioral effect will be nearly impossible to change. The good news is, it does not have to be difficult.

At first glance, blaming substances and circumstances appears logical. While there are certain physical circumstances you cannot change, like your height or missing limbs, there are people who have these same handicaps who live happy and successful lives.

Basketball star Tyrone "Muggsy" Bogues did not let his height of five foot three inches limit his ability to have a long and successful career in the NBA from 1987 to 2001. During one of those seasons, he played alongside one of the tallest players in the NBA, who was twenty-eight inches taller!

Helen Keller became a famous author and speaker despite being a blind, deaf, and mute child. What really matters is not what is, but rather what you believe about what is. What you believe about your circumstances directly affects what you do with them.

What Is Real?

We do not operate from the real world. We operate from our *perception* of the world. This idea is far more literal than most people understand. It may sound like just another platitude, but look a little deeper.

Your mind operates like a computer. When you are born, your brain is completely empty. From day one, your brain records every sight, sound, taste, smell, movement, feeling, interaction, and chemical reaction you experience. You may think you don't have a good memory, but everything you have ever experienced has been recorded through your five senses and stored in your neurology. The shorthand that your mind/body system uses to store, sort and encode all those experiences is emotion.

When I ask people where they were on the morning of September 11, 2001, almost everyone can state exactly where they were and what they were doing when those planes hit the twin towers in New York City. When I ask them where they were on the morning of May 11, 2001, they have no idea. What makes one day more memorable than another? Emotion! You don't struggle to remember your birthday because there is emotion attached to it.

Humans are meaning-making machines. Every time a new experience comes along, your mind stores it with emotion. If the emotion is weak or neutral, you might save it as a less important file. If you felt fantastic during a new experience, your mind night store that event in a file called, "I need to do this as often as possible, no matter what!" If you have a new experience with a strong negative emotion, you may save that file as, "Urgent, my survival depends on never experiencing this again!" If you never counter or reframe the negative emotions in that experience, then from that point forward, your unconscious mind will develop behaviors to avoid anything like it for the rest of your life. Over time, those behaviors, originally meant to keep you safe, can become so extreme that they actually hurt you. This happens long before you are old enough to apply logic or reason to the process.

I once saw a client who was very depressed. After a few questions, I discovered she had a belief that no one cared about what she thought. She had a lifetime of proof where people pushed her to do things before she was ready, and they regularly disregarded her opinion. She especially had problems with doctors and was embroiled in her third malpractice lawsuit. I kept taking her back farther and farther into her childhood, trying to find the first incidence where this pattern started. We cleared memories from college, high school, and elementary school. Finally, I said, "Tell me about your birth." She became defensive and said, "There was nothing wrong with my birth. I was born to young parents who wanted me and loved me. My birth was great. Except ..."

I thought to myself, here it comes!

She continued, "My mother did tell me that the doctor was in a hurry to get to his golf game and pulled me out with forceps." And there it was. Her birth experience and the story around it had set up a lifelong pattern of emotional reactions toward doctors, as well as anyone who snubbed her desires and opinions. We used FasterEFT to clear the negative emotions and create new meaning around her birth experience. Now, her whole life has changed.

How Mind Body Communication Works

When you come into this world, your new brain records every experience. With each new experience, your brain searches its memory banks, looking for similar references to determine how it should react. When very young children who are just learning to walk fall down, they often look up at the adult to see how they should react. If the parent freaks out, the child mirrors their behavior by crying. Sometimes, the parent can make a silly remark like "Oopsy" and scoop up the child causing it to giggle instead of cry. This simple act can teach the child's brain that it is okay to fall down occasionally, get up happy, and continue playing.

Whenever something happens to a child and its brain searches for and finds a memory with a similar aspect, it automatically groups those experiences together. Over time, the child's brain gradually creates a file of mental and emotional resources on every topic.

You have built a mental and emotional resource library for every issue and circumstance in your life. Those files are the building blocks of your beliefs. Once your brain has assigned meaning to your past experiences, the past then generates the meaning of all similar experiences for the rest of your life, unless you actively do something to change that pre-established meaning.

For example, if your first encounter with a snake terrified you, those emotions will remain with you for the rest of your life, unless you change your primary reference at the level of your subconscious mind. The bigger your mental resource file on any subject, the more proof you have that a belief is real or true. No matter how large your internal resource, FasterEFT can change it by interrupting the mind/body communication, which allows the body to relax so the unconscious mind can create new mental resources.

Your Map Of The World

Your life experience creates the mental resources that generate your individual map of the world. Your map is not a map of what is actually true, because, technically speaking, there is no such thing. Ten people can witness the same event and walk away with ten different truths about what actually happened. Ask any police officer who has interviewed members of a crowd who witnessed a crime. They will tell you, no two people have exactly the same story. That's because, in the words of psychologist and best-selling author Dr. Wayne Dyer, we don't believe what we see, we see what we believe.

Is The Past Real?

The past was real when it happened. And your reaction to what happened was definitely real at the time. But it is not real *now* because it is no longer happening, unless you recreate it in your mind. If the past is no longer real, and you are still suffering from what happened back then, what's happening? Who is doing it to you now? Inside your mind, you are the movie director, the perpetrator, the victim, and the bystanders. There is no one else inside your head but you. Therefore, you, and only you, have the power to control what happens on the mental screen of your mind.

The future is not real either. It has not happened yet. You rely on past experiences to guide your expectations, but the future has not happened. What you believe to be true about your now tends to become your future. What you believe is possible tends to show up for you. This present moment is all you really have. And all your power is right here in the present.

Reality Versus Fantasy
Have you ever gone to a really good movie and lost yourself so completely that you felt intense emotions, as if they were real? Or have you ever read a book that was so absorbing that you felt anger, heat, cold, fear, sadness, or just laughed out loud? What made you feel those feelings? Was it the print on the page? Or the image on the screen? Of course not. It all happened inside your mind. The words and images triggered your mental resources, producing a feeling in your body as if it was real, even when it was made up.

Your conscious mind does not care if you are biting into a lemon or simply imagining it. Either way, your body can produce the same physical response of puckering and increasing saliva. Your body cannot distinguish between watching a very sad movie and finding out that someone you know died. Both events can cause your eyes to produce physical tears. The meaning you give to those two events will be very different, but the physical response can be exactly the same. Your mind and body are one system and that system is always serving you. You can take responsibility and direct it, or you can sit back and become a victim. The choice is entirely up to you.

World class athletes understand this more than most. At the level of the Olympics, the difference between first and second place can be as small as hundredths of a second. Athletes know that they have to use every resource available to win. They learn from world class coaches how to engage their mind to support their goals. Mental rehearsal is the secret ingredient to winning. And, it's also the secret ingredient to losing!

How often do you think about aspects of your life being difficult or impossible? And how often do you tell yourself that you are a genius and a winner? All you have to do is look at your results in life and the answers to those two questions will become obvious.

Successful people have a predominance of happy, successful thoughts while unsuccessful and unhappy people have a predominance of sad, fearful, angry, guilty, unworthy, and other negative thoughts. In fact, most of us spend hours, even years, rehearsing the bad stuff we don't want. And we wonder why we keep attracting more of it.

I had a client who wanted to improve his golf score. He told me he had a wicked left hook that he could not correct, no matter how hard he tried. I asked him to tell me everything he thought, said, and did as he prepared to play golf. Every time he approached the ball, moved into position, and prepared to swing, he thought, "I am *not* going to hook this one."

As he thought about what he did not want, he visualized and prepared for what he did not want. He visualized the hook before the swing and, as a result, he successfully hooked it almost every time.

I showed him that his problem was actually a success. He was actively thinking his problem into being. His unconscious mind served up his deeply embedded belief that he almost always hooked the ball and that became his self fulfilling prophecy.

I tapped on the golfer to eliminate his past references for anxiety, disappointment, anger, embarrassment, and frustration. Once we cleared the negative emotions, I asked him to imagine how he would like the golf ball to behave. He rehearsed his dream shot over and over in his mind. He saw the ball going straight down the fairway, farther than ever before. He imagined hearing the sound of his buddies shouting, "Wow! Amazing!" He saw them showering him with high fives.

I then had him hold an actual golf club, step into position, close his eyes and mentally rehearse his awesome swing. I asked him to hear the crack of the club face hitting the ball, see the perfect, long, straight flight of the ball and the awed reactions of everyone around him. We did this over and over as we tapped in the new positive outcome. I asked him to do this every night before he fell asleep and when he woke up, before he left his house to play golf, and while he was on the course.

In two weeks, he radically improved his swing and his score. He was ecstatic. By taking ownership of his mind and putting it to work on what he wanted, instead of what he did not want, he was able to change his old pattern. He expended some effort to retrain his habitual thinking, but the rewards were exciting and fun.

Athletes in every sport know the power of mental rehearsal plus physical practice. And when you add tapping to the mix, it supercharges your efforts. If you apply this powerful tool to the circumstances and emotions in your life, you will reap the rewards of success, joy, love, and freedom. When you take ownership of your mind, you rule your life.

STEP FOUR EXERCISES

Mind Movies

Notice the kind of mental movies that regularly play in your mind. Have you been playing horror movies, suspense movies, or dark comedies in your head? Are they working for you?

- Create a movie in your mind of something you want to accomplish. It can be something you have never done before or something you would like to improve. For example, public speaking, exercise, loving relationships, pushing away from the table when you are full, or enjoying a glass of water with lemon, instead of a sugary soft drink. Imagine the entire scenario and include the following steps:

  - Prepare for the activity. With exercise, you would put on your gym shoes.

  - Go to the place where it will happen. For example, imagine driving to the gym.

  - Set it up. Get on the machine and set the weight.

  - Do it in a fantastic way. See yourself pumping iron.

  - Celebrate your successful completion. Imagine seeing yourself in the mirror in great shape. Add positive feelings, sensations, and emotions at each step along the way. You may imagine yourself on a treadmill, listening to music. Perspiration rolls down your back. Hear the sounds of weights clanking. Feel the excitement, the hugs, the high fives of your friends. Experience the joy of accomplishment, whatever is appropriate for your movie.

- Note: If you feel that this is stupid or useless, tap on that feeling and release it.

- Once you have created your movie in your mind, play it over and over until it feels absolutely real. Play it in your mind before you go to sleep, when you first wake up in the morning, and as many times during the day as possible. Tap in the good feelings as you imagine your successful mind movie.

- Do this until your mental movie becomes a physical reality.

- Reward yourself for taking control of your life.

STEP FIVE

RELEASE THE PAIN AND HURT

Without freedom from the past, there is no freedom at all.

~Krishnamurti

Something interesting occurred in my neighborhood recently involving the housing market. Two houses, built by the same builder, in the same year, with the same square footage, were listed for almost the exact same price. Both homes are lovely, well-maintained and have a view. The couple up the street put a big sign in their yard and immediately started telling their neighbors stories about how depressed the market is right now and how they *hope* they can sell their house. The couple down the street did not tell anyone they were selling. They did not even put a sign in their yard because three days after they listed, they received a cash offer, slightly above asking price, from a couple who wanted to close as soon as possible. The house up the street stayed on the market for four months. Only three people came to see it. Feeling stuck, they took it off the market for the holidays and said they would *try* to re-list it next year.

I was stuck for a very long time in the belief that I was stuck. I believed in the truth of outside circumstances more than I believed in the idea that all I needed was already within me. I received great training for this false belief from family members, friends, teachers, religious leaders and of course, the media. And I practiced being stuck for decades. I successfully and consistently manifested my limiting beliefs. As I look back on that time, I realize that every circumstance I found myself in was a reflection of something I held to be true, consciously or unconsciously.

I watched other people with enormous frustration as they obtained very different outcomes than I was experiencing. Sometimes, it even made me angry that they could have the things I wanted but believed were difficult or nearly impossible to achieve. And when they did it with relative ease and lots of joy… How dare they!

The only difference between the two houses on my street is the owners. One couple appears to live a charmed life, in business as well as their personal lives. The other couple does not. I began to ask myself, why does this happen? I know both couples and I can say, without a doubt, they have very different views of the world because they come from different life experiences and beliefs. (Remember, our experiences, and the meanings we give them, are the building blocks of our beliefs.)

The couple who did not sell their house has what they refer to as "serious problems that will never go away." These problems are not just affecting them financially. They are having serious repercussions in their family relationships, their physical health, and their social life. The couple who sold their house in three days for more than asking price are fit, healthy, happy, have loads of friends, happy kids, and they are thriving. You can call it luck and dismiss it or you can look a little deeper for clues based on their beliefs and their results. But in the end, success and happiness depend not so much on what happens to us, but on how we react to and deal with what happens.

Most coaches and experts will tell you that if you want a certain outcome, emulate someone who already achieves those results. Find out what they think, say, do, feel and believe. Results are feedback. They are not an excuse to beat yourself up, or blame others, or even to celebrate. They are simply feedback. Results can be harsh. But they are always fair. Because results are effects, not causes.

Results can sometimes appear random and confusing. We see what we don't like in our experience and we blame those circumstances for our problems. Circumstances, like results, are just feedback. If you find yourself in the same undesirable circumstances that your parents were in, then it's a possibility that you bought your parents beliefs about what is normal. Instead of settling for your family's beliefs, you can choose to let their old beliefs go and create new ones, which will then create new circumstances for you.

Wayne Dyer has said many times, "You'll see it when you believe it, not the other way around."[8] Most of us learned the exact opposite as children. It's time to release your old beliefs and embrace something new. Are your old beliefs creating joyous miracles for you? If so, you should keep them. If not, consider changing them.

Do I Have To Release The Old First?

The truth is, you do not have to spend any time releasing the old negative beliefs. Technically, you are a magnificent spiritual being that has the power and the presence to simply decide to be, do and have something different. And don't ever let anyone tell otherwise. Right here, right now, you have the power to heal or change anything! Jesus did it and said you have the power to do this and even greater things.

There are thousands of stories of miraculous healings of all kinds. And not just in biblical times, but today. There are amazing, medically documented stories about people quickly and mysteriously cured of cancer and other serious illnesses. We call them miracles because they are few and far between.

Why are miracles so rare? If they exist, and they do, why aren't they reproducible? Why don't we take a good hard look at what caused those spontaneous remissions, figure out what really happened and then reproduce them in others? That would be the scientific approach, wouldn't it? Most doctors will not even investigate a spontaneous remission out of fear of being labeled a crack pot. They call it an *anomaly* and dismiss it immediately. Allopathic medicine tends to focus only on the disease, not on the healing.

We are all trained from an early age to focus on what went wrong. When something goes right, we say, "What luck!" Then we turn away and look for another problem to solve. For people who have a strong personal connection to problem solving, I recommend that you try FasterEFT tapping.

As you begin to heal and release your hurts and pains, you will simultaneously be adding proofs to your unconscious mind about your power to heal yourself. And, you will also be simultaneously building a

---

8   Dyer, Wayne W. *You'll See It When You Believe It.* New York: W. Morrow, 1989. Print.

new belief system, which will automatically create a whole new world around you.

Robert Smith, the founder and creator of FasterEFT says "Tap for the rest of your life, even on your death bed." And that is good advice. After just a few years of tapping, I can see how it has been retraining my mind to respond differently. Things that used to make me crazy, now make me laugh. Instead of cursing at a person who cuts me off in traffic, I bless them. Now, I almost never encounter people who cut me off unless I am entertaining some other negativity in my own mind. So when they cut me off, I bless them and start tapping on me. I can give my power over to the problem, or I can take ownership and put the power back where it belongs—inside me.

That is what I call enlightenment. I have an idea that if I tapped enough and cleared absolutely every negative event and emotion, I could eventually become like one of those enlightened people and I would not need to tap any more. Except, life keeps happening. So until I and everyone else on the planet is operating from pure love and nothing else, I'll just keep tapping. Tapping is my new coping mechanism. And it can be yours too.

Creating A Strong Foundation

Releasing your hurt and pain leads you to a greater sense of peace, trust, joy and freedom. Trying to create a fabulous life from a place of intense pain and suffering is like trying to build on quicksand. If you were raised by people who hurt you or if you have had encounters with people who hurt you, that can produce a pattern of you hurting yourself. Holding onto your pain makes it difficult for you to believe in the goodness, power and freedom that is always available to you.

If you find yourself with a mind full of pain and hurt, then please, recognize that you are where you are. It does no good to blame others or shame yourself. Take ownership of your life and start tapping on everything that bothers you. Tap for yourself. Tap for the people you love. Tap for the people who have to deal with you every day.

Hurt people, hurt people. That's right. Hurt people are the ones who hurt people. If you are hurting, there is a good chance your pain will eventually explode outward onto someone else. It may be in the form of an argument, or a slap or worse. It certainly explodes inwardly on you. Those hurts inside are what make you want to drink, do drugs, overeat, gamble, spend too much money, get sick, and a long list of other behaviors caused by fear and pain. Release the hurt inside you, and you will stop hurting yourself and others.

If someone hurt you, it's pretty much a certainty that, at some point, someone hurt them. It is also likely that they were hurt in the same way they hurt you. It's how they learned to do it. And they have now taught you how to hurt yourself, and others. All you have to do is think about how they hurt you and it's like they are doing it to you all over again. In reality, they are not doing it to you *anymore*. Who is doing it to you now? You are! By holding onto those painful memories and replaying them over and over, you are now the perpetrator. You are hurting you, using the great power of your own mind.

But as you consciously step into your power and learn how to let go of the pain, you gain the freedom of never having to be the victim again, and you become capable of creating a whole new way of being. Imagine living without all that pain and hurt. Only you can make that decision. Only you can choose to release your pain and create a new foundation that will support a life you love living. Only you have that power.

Does Pain Make You Smarter?

I have had clients who wanted to stop their session just as they were letting go of a huge problem. They think they can't let go of what happened because they need that information to protect them from other people who might hurt them. This is a completely false idea.

Some people have a pathological fear of rattle snakes. All they have to do is imagine one, and they can have a full-blown panic attack, even if there are no rattlesnakes within a hundred miles. Panic attacks are a powerful use of the mind body connection.

Imagine the opposite of a panic attack. What if you could think about being totally confident and instantly walk out on stage and speak to a crowd of thousands without any nervousness? If your mind can produce instant panic, it can produce instant confidence. Which one are you practicing?

Panic attacks unleash a flood of stress hormones that can cause real physical damage to your body. Reliving traumatic events in your mind on a regular basis takes an enormous toll on your physical and mental well-being.

By using FasterEFT and tapping on the emotions, you can release the panic response and feel totally comfortable and at peace looking at a rattlesnake. However, if you are out hiking, you will *not* want to go over and pick one up and cuddle it. Releasing your fears does not make you stupid. It makes you smarter. You release the fear and keep the wisdom. You will still understand and respect that rattlesnakes are poisonous and you will naturally give it a safe distance. But you will not have to suffer from the adrenaline rush and emotional overload of a panic attack.

Any fireman or police officer will tell you that people who are terrified become completely stupid. They run toward danger instead of away from it. People in fear do stupid things that hurt themselves, and hurt others in the process. A drowning person will grab onto a lifeguard who is trying to save them and pull them under. That's why lifeguards carry a float for the drowning person to grab, then they can drag them to shore safely.

When you release your fears, hurts, angers, sadness, shame, disappointment, apathy and every other negative emotion, you actually become smarter. You suddenly have resources you didn't even know you had. Miracles begin to happen. As the contents of your conscious and subconscious mind changes, so do your circumstances, your body, your finances, your relationships, and everything else.

Call it a miracle. Or call it the way things work. Just start where you are and tap your way to the tipping point—away from the downward spiral of pain and hurt and into the upward spiral of joy and success.

Life produces results, and results are just feedback. Notice where you are. Take ownership by stepping into your power. Seek wisdom and apply it so you can begin to develop positive inner communication skills. As you work on your inner communication skills, you will discover the amazing connection between your mind and body, your thoughts and circumstances, and you will find yourself releasing the past and moving into the next step, which is finding peace within you.

STEP FIVE EXERCISES

Tapping
Apply FasterEFT Tapping to your Peace List.
- Release all the negative emotions in each and every negative memory in your entire life. Tap until you completely let it go.

- If you have been a member of a traditional twelve step program, use your fourth step inventory as your Peace List and tap away all the pain and suffering, fear and shame, powerlessness and guilt.

- Create a small group of people who will support you and each other as you work through your Peace List.

STEP SIX

MAKE PEACE INSIDE EVERY MEMORY

We define ourselves by the best that is in us, not the worst that has been done to us.

~Edward Lewis

Let us now live out of our imagination instead of our memory.

~Les Brown

When I was eleven years old, I witnessed the aftermath of a terrible crime. A man was attacked and badly beaten by a deranged assailant less than a block from our home. After a harrowing ordeal, he escaped and sought safety at the nearest house with a light on. Our house was empty except for me, my younger sister and our childhood caregiver, Becky, who was cleaning the kitchen. The shock of seeing this bloody and battered stranger at our back door was traumatic. I froze and became speechless, while my younger sister threw up at the sight of him.

After the ambulance came and took the man to the hospital, the gravity of that situation and all of its ramifications were permanently imprinted deep in my unconscious mind.

Memory is a tricky thing. I am not exactly sure what I saw that night because apparently my memory has changed over the years. I recently asked my younger sister what she saw and our two memories were slightly different. My memory was of this stranger crawling through the back door on his hands and knees while my sister remembered him leaning on the door bell outside the sliding glass door to our kitchen. In reality, neither of us saw the man enter the house. We both *constructed* memories of his arrival from things we heard later on. What really happened was, Becky brought us downstairs to "See what happens to people who roam the streets at night." The stranger was not at the door when we saw him. He was in horrible shape, but he was sitting at our kitchen table, waiting for the police and ambulance to arrive.

Becky must have sincerely believed that if we saw someone battered and bloody, it would help us to behave responsibly and keep us safe in the future. That may sound like a ridiculous thing to show two children. However, Becky was old enough to remember the terrible story of the kidnapping and death of famous aviator Charles Lindbergh's baby. I remember her talking about it and expressing fear that my sister and I, the children of her famous employer (my mother), could be the target of a kidnapper. She always kept a close eye on us. I can only imagine that she was prepared to do anything to keep us safe on her watch. Looking back on it, my life would probably have been quite different without that particular lesson, but what I know now is that she was doing the best she could with the information she had at the time.

Unfortunately, that horrible memory grew and changed inside my young mind as I tried to make sense of it and give it appropriate meaning. Eventually, my unconscious mind combined what I actually saw with snippets of information I overheard from adults, both at home and on the news. I was not present at the crime scene. I did not see any of it. But I did create a picture inside my head of some of the horrible things I heard. In an attempt to understand what had happened, my young mind made up a horror movie and I used that completely made up "memory" as if it was real to scare myself for decades.

As I carried those images inside me, both the real and the fabricated memories, I experienced a constant level of anxiety and felt that I had to be looking over my shoulder at all times to make sure no one was coming to attack me. My unconscious mind used my strong *emotions* and strong visual *proof* to create a *belief* that the world was not a safe place. My *true* belief affected *everything* in my life. I avoided doing anything that would bring attention to myself, which makes it difficult to succeed. For me, being a success was dangerous. Having money, talent, a position of influence, or even just being thin and attractive made me very, very uncomfortable.

My feelings and actions were not logical or rational. Rather, it was as if some unseen force was constantly messing with my plans and my life. As soon as I started to succeed at something, I would either sabotage it or quit. As soon as someone wanted to be my friend, I would do something to offend them. I flipped back and forth between apathy and hating myself. Illness became a regular preoccupation. All those years, I could not understand what was wrong with me. But now, I can see that my unconscious mind was going to great lengths to avoid the horror I was holding inside my own mind.

One of the most radical ideas I have ever come across is the idea that memories can be changed. If you mention changing memories to anyone in the academic psychological community, they might assume that you were trying to avoid facing the truth; that you were living in denial. Most people call denial unhealthy. And if you were simply burying bad memories, then I would completely agree. That is not what I am talking about. Changing your memories involves facing them, but not in the traditional talk therapy model or the storytelling model of the traditional twelve step meeting.

The process of FasterEFT involves *going there* for the last time. You do not have to visit the old pain over and over again every week for twenty years. Some painful memories can be addressed and transformed in as little as ten minutes. Some of the bigger, more horrible and more practiced memories can be transformed in one two-hour session. When there are many different memories of the same problem, for instance, years of repeated abuse, it may take many sessions to eliminate all the parts and pieces. But there will be relief along the way as each memory is transformed and new meaning is created. It also depends on how willing you are to participate in the process. You must be honest and you must want it. If there are emotions in the way, like not feeling worthy of a healing or too much shame and blame, those emotions can be easily dealt with so you can then find the root of your problem and pull it out, once and for all.

Occasionally, a client will stop me midsession and ask if it's okay to change a bad memory. One woman even joked that the "reality police" might descend on her and lock her up for letting go of her painful past. Her identity was objecting to the process of letting it go. Memories are the building blocks we use to create our identity. We believe that we are our memories. We believe we are our past. If we change our past, who will we be? Generally speaking, if you let go of your bad memories, you will still be you, just happier and more successful.

The only problem that can occur with letting it all go happens when other people — especially family members — don't want to let go of your past. But if you persist, your whole world will eventually change and they will either accept the new you or your worlds will stop colliding. You will become like magnets at opposite poles that just cannot seem to come together. Or you will only come together when their mental atmosphere is at the same level as yours; either when yours dips, or when theirs comes up.

Sometimes my clients think if they let go of how they were attacked or abused, it will make them vulnerable, and they will become victims of other people who want to harm them. But the exact opposite is true. Whatever you hold within, especially if you rehearse it in your mind often enough, will eventually reproduce itself into your reality.

Looking back on my childhood, it's no longer a surprise to me that I was bullied during eighth grade. Just two years before that, at eleven years old, my brain created the strong belief that I was constantly vulnerable to being attacked by any random stranger on the street. I had real proof that being attacked was possible. In addition, my mother was a celebrity, so my young mind naturally assumed that to be successful and please my family, I should also be a star. Combine the mental program that wants to be a star with the mental program that constantly fears attack and what do you get? Bullying! Interesting. I created being a star in a negative way.

Memories Are Generative
Another radical concept that Law of Attraction promoters have been tossing around for some time is "You get what you think about most." I had accepted this idea, but no one ever explained it to me as clearly as Robert Smith's FasterEFT philosophy.

> *It is not the events of our lives that continue to bother us long after they are over. It is how we process and internalize those events.*

Another way to say that is, it's not the event, but the meaning we give it that colors our lives. And meaning is created by how we represent our experiences internally.

All internal representations are memories. A feeling is a memory. Even a smell is a memory. If smells were not recorded in your memory, you would have to re-learn them every time you smelled the same odor.

Your memories build the mental programs that run your life, whether you realize it or not. To give you an example from my own experience, my two most significant negative memories — witnessing the aftermath of that terrible crime at eleven and then getting bullied at thirteen — were running my life and keeping me stuck in a deep rut of fear, loneliness, failure, and despair. I lived in complete fear and mistrust of all people. I even stopped trusting and believing in God. I was highly suspicious of anyone who said they wanted to be my friend. And romance (even though my conscious mind really wanted it) was completely out of the question. Every time I had the possibility of a love interest, I sabotaged it before it could start. My body responded by growing bigger and bigger while my world got smaller and smaller. My unconscious mind loved me so much that it made me fat and lonely so I could be safe.

Being miserable and lonely was the only way my unconscious mind could cope with its need to feel safe. I was a child when these experiences happened. My parents and teachers did not have great emotional skills. I did the best I could. It was a real wakeup call when I finally realized that all my fears, my addictions, and my often senseless behaviors were based in love. That can be hard to see when senseless behavior is happening and it feels terrible. It's shocking to think that sticking a needle full of heroin into your arm could be an act of love. But in my experience, it always is. Out of love, the unconscious mind will do anything to keep a person from experiencing those painful emotions. Wouldn't it be nice to have a better coping mechanism?

We are not born with a user's manual for our brain. Scientists still disagree about exactly how the brain works. But since the 1990's, a lot more information has become available about how our mind and body work together to create our life. The new science of neuroplasticity is pointing us all to new knowledge and new possibilities.

When I discovered FasterEFT on YouTube (www.YouTube.com/HealingMagic), I saw people tapping away memories that were much worse than mine and seeing their whole lives change right before my eyes. I thought to myself, "I want that!" So I called Robert Smith, the creator of FasterEFT. He was still taking clients back then. I booked a one hour phone session with him and during that hour, we completely released the negative emotions in my two most painful memories: seeing that battered man and the bullying in eighth grade. But he did not stop there. The FasterEFT philosophy teaches that releasing the negative emotions is only *part one* of the process. To make deep and lasting change, you have to transform or "flip" the memory, after removing the negative emotion. This often happens automatically.

Imagine walking down the street and someone slams into you, knocking you off balance and you spill a cup of coffee all over yourself. Your first reaction is anger. What idiot is not paying attention to where they are going! Then in the next second, you see that the person is blind. He apologizes. In an instant, the entire "memory" reframes itself. Now it has a completely different meaning. You easily let go of your anger and perhaps you have a short conversation. Or maybe you help the blind person reorient themselves to where they were going. Now, that event, which started out negative is suddenly something you feel good about. Flipping a memory means you are giving it new resources and new meaning.

When I work with clients, they are often surprised as we tap away the negative emotions. More than a few clients have given me a confused look and said something like "This is so strange ... My father is not beating me anymore. He's taking me by the hand and we're going to the zoo."

What if that were possible with all your memories? Even your worst, most horrible memories? I am here to tell you that it is. And, creating new meaning around the events of your life will completely change your present experience and dramatically change your future. It certainly changed mine.

After releasing all the negative emotions out of my worst memories of being bullied in eighth grade, Robert Smith asked me, "So, what would you rather have had happen to you in eighth grade?" That question threw me. "What? What do you mean?" He asked again. "What would you have liked to experience in eighth grade?" That thought had never occurred to me. I searched my mind and came up blank. I had no resources for such an idea. So he asked me "Where's a place you felt safe and happy when you were thirteen?" I had taken over the basement of our family home and turned it into my art studio. I painted scenes on all the walls and made it cozy with yard furniture, an old sofa, and pillows. Together, Robert and I created a *new* memory of me standing on that old sofa with all the kids from eighth grade sitting on the floor looking up at me, smiling and laughing, as I told jokes and stories. I don't know what made me create that exact scene. My unconscious mind just served it up and it felt good. So we tapped it into my unconscious mind. Now, whenever I think about eighth grade, (which is not nearly as often as I used to), I see the new positive memory instead of the old one of boys spitting on me and girls not talking to me. I can't really remember those events anymore. Technically, I know they are facts that happened, but I don't see them and I can't feel them or get upset about them anymore. My new *made up* memory is now more real to me than what *really* happened. I have a new reference; a new internal resource. One I didn't have before.

I admit that sounds strange the first time you hear it. I used to find it shocking. Making up memories … isn't that being delusional? Also known as insane? I think the key is, are you first, releasing the negative emotions and second, doing it with conscious intension? Or are you attempting to bury or escape from a negative emotion? Is your mind running away with you or are you in charge of your thoughts?

Why Would You Want To Change Your Memories?

For decades, every time I talked about eighth grade, I became choked up and emotional. Now when I think about eighth grade, I smile and laugh. There is peace and joy inside me, where once there was only fear, anger and sadness. How could that change so quickly and easily? That fear, anger, and sadness is what drove my addiction. Now that I have released the negative emotions and transformed my perceptions, my addictive behavior has also been transformed. This is the miracle of FasterEFT. It works within the system of how the mind naturally works. And now I help others transform their memories and change their lives.

For as long as I can remember, I have been terrified of public speaking. Even standing up in front of a small group of five friends to tell a story traumatized me. My voice shook, my throat got dry and felt like it was closing up, my stomach tensed, and my whole body started to sweat profusely. I felt like my body was betraying me as these symptoms spiraled out of control. The anxiety in my body reflected the covert need of my unconscious mind to protect me—at all costs.

I'll give you an example of how unconscious trances controlled me using my body. The afternoon before my older sister got married, I was told that, as the maid of honor, I should stand up and give a toast at her rehearsal dinner. Within an hour, I was so sick I was bedridden and I missed the dinner. For the wedding the next day, I was well. My fever and other symptoms were absolutely real. I did not pretend to be sick. In fact, I was very upset about missing a great party. Everyone assumed I had some strange twenty-four hour flu. And I was equally mystified. It never occurred to me that my unconscious mind was playing a trick on me for any purpose, let alone to keep me safe!

Another interesting effect of my FasterEFT session with Robert Smith where I created a made up memory of having fun telling jokes to an audience, I literally woke up one morning and thought, "I'd like to be a public speaker." And now, I can't get enough of being on stage or speaking to groups. I even joined Toastmasters to have more stage time! I never worked on or tapped on my fear of public speaking. The root cause was simply gone. I now have a made up memory of standing on that old sofa talking to kids I used to think hated me. My new memory focuses on having fun inside my mind! Memories are actually generative. Your memories generate your beliefs, which generate your present and your future. This is what I mean when I say: "What you hold within, shows up in your life."

So what are you holding onto that you would like to have less of? And how would you rather remember that time in your life? What would you rather have experienced? Go ahead. Make it up. It is your brain and it is your life. You get to choose. In fact, you are choosing right now, whether you are aware of it or not. You are either choosing to keep the pain and suffering and push it down with some addiction, or you are choosing to do something new. The power is within you now.

The greatest gift that humankind has ever been given is free will. The ultimate freedom is to choose exactly what we think about everything and everyone. The happiest and most successful people on Earth are the ones who choose memories and meanings that serve them, instead of ones that hurt them.

There is a wonderful story about two little girls. One is an optimist, always focusing on the good, and one is a pessimist, always focusing on the bad. Their parents decided to test them one Christmas by filling the little pessimist's room with gifts and putting a giant pile of horse manure in the little optimist's room. On Christmas morning, the little pessimist opened all her presents and was happy for a short while. But then, she started to find faults with all her gifts and complained that she didn't get what she really wanted. The little optimist came running out of her room extremely excited and shouting "Where is it? Where is it?" The parents asked her "Where is what?" And the little optimist said "With all that poop, there has to be a pony around here somewhere!"

Ok, it is just a cute story, but which one are you? The rest of your life will be guided by your choice, so choose wisely. Choose consciously. And if you don't like the results you have been getting, figure out what beliefs you need to change to achieve a different result.

Memories Are Not Real

People get upset when I say that. I do not mean to invalidate your life experience. What happened to you absolutely happened. It was real when it happened. But the best thing about the past is, it's over now. It is not happening any more, unless you actively re-create it in your own mind.

Memories are imperfect at best. Do you have a memory that you can close your eyes and see? Do you have one where you can see everyone in the memory, including yourself? Most of us do. It's called seeing in the third person. Well, guess what? That is not possible. Your brain edited that memory. You were not a fly on the ceiling looking down at what was happening to you. You cannot see the back of your head right now, can you? That memory is made up. Your mind rearranged the memory according to your beliefs. Yes, that painful thing really happened. It was real back then. But it is not real now. To experience it as real now, you must re-create a sad, painful movie of it in your mind.

Memories seem like they are still happening because of the strong emotions which trigger real bodily reactions when you think of them. Remember how just thinking about biting into a lemon can trigger increased saliva production in your mouth? How about looking at porn? People spend billions of dollars annually to look at pictures that trigger a real physical response in their body. No one is there. It is just an illusion on a screen. But the power of the mind makes it real by triggering internal references, which trigger real emotions, which create very real expressions in the body. I once heard a sex therapist state that the largest and most important sex organ is the brain. All cravings and compulsions are based on memories and how you internally represent them.

Internal References

We cannot experience things in our life that we have no reference for. To illustrate this point, there is a famous story written by one of the earliest explorers of the New World. When his men rowed to shore and got out of their small boats, the Native Americans could see them, but they wanted to know where they had come from. Apparently, they could not see the large sailing ships anchored in the harbor because they had no reference for them. So they called in the tribal spiritual leader who came to understand the concept of large vessels sailing across the sea. The spiritual leader eventually saw the large ships, then created a story to tell to his people to give them a reference for the ships. Only after they had an internal reference could they actually see the ships in the harbor.

That is an extreme example involving an isolated tribe of people living an ancient ancestral lifestyle. Today, with the internet, it's hard to believe that a person could not see or even imagine something new and different. But it happens all the time.

British illusionist, Darren Brown, performs amazing tricks that shine a light on how our beliefs and perceptions literally control what we can and cannot see. He once met a man who believed so strongly in his own constant misfortune that he could not see a real opportunity if it was right in front of him. He set out to prove his point with a film crew in tow. He followed this guy around for days putting good fortune directly in his path. He had someone place a fifty pound note (about seventy-five dollars) on the sidewalk a block from his work. He walked right past it. They put all manner of good fortune and amazing opportunities in his direct path, but day after day, he acted as if nothing was there.

I once met a guy in Silicon Valley who grew up very poor. He was a software engineer, employed in a field where his colleagues were making very high salaries. But he always appeared to be broke, driving a beat up old van and complaining that he could not pay his rent. His friends could not understand how he was not thriving like they were. He was raised without a reference for success. And having a scientific mind, he believed in what he knew. He bought into the idea that struggle and poverty were real. He also knew that while success and abundance might actually exist, it was not real for him. What he did not realize was, his brain was capable of creating a new internal reference that could substantially transform his reality. And you can too.

In my own life, I knew there must be people out there who could eat without an internal battle of obsession, guilt, and self-loathing. I have seen people enjoying food and having healthy fit bodies. But it was never something I believed could be real for me. I just did not know how to create it. My subconscious beliefs were running me. I had thousands, maybe even millions of references for being fat, out of control, helpless, not deserving and a victim. I had no internal reference for being thin and fit.

I used to get mad at myself for losing fifty pounds, then gaining back what I had worked so hard to lose. Especially when I suddenly realized, I forgot to take a picture of myself when I was at my thinnest. Because I had no internal reference for me being thin, I never even took a photograph of myself when I was thin for a fleeting moment. I did that not once, but over and over again.

Internal References - How We Store Memories

The mind body system uses the five senses to make our experiences feel real. These five modalities are: Visual (what you see), Auditory (what you hear), Kinesthetic (what you feel), Olfactory (what you smell) and Gustatory (what you taste). Within these five modalities are a variety of submodalities that include, but are not limited to:

Visual	Auditory	Kinesthetic	Olfactory	Gustatory
Black & White	Loud or Soft	Location	Strong or Mild	Sweet
Color	High or Low	Size	Familiar or Not	Sour
Bright or Dim	Fast or Slow	Duration	Fresh	Salty
Location	Interior/Exterior	Intensity 0-10	Putrid	Savory
Size of Image	Direction	Pressure	Burnt	Bitter
Still or Movie	Uniqueness	Temperature	Smells like…	Tastes like…

When you close your eyes and go back to a memory, you re-experience that memory through submodalities. Your brain stores and cross references memories using submodalities. The easiest way to change a memory is to simply imagine it, then change the submodalities as if you were changing the settings on a television or computer screen. This is the exact process I used to give up a five to six cup a day coffee habit in just ten minutes, with zero withdrawals and no side effects.

Here's How I Quit My Coffee Addiction

FasterEFT and NLP both utilize your natural mental system of storing references (or memories) called submodalities. Here are the details outlining how I completely gave up coffee in ten minutes using only the power of that mental system.

First, I imagined a happy picture of me drinking coffee. I visualized myself and my husband sitting up in bed on a Saturday morning drinking coffee with our dog resting between us. The picture was bright. It was as if I were looking out through my own eyes. I was not seeing me, just my husband and my dog and the coffee. It was a movie. It was right out in front of my face as I imagined it with my eyes closed.

Next, I imagined a picture of something I hated drinking. I was at a health event where someone suggested I drink a shot glass of wheatgrass juice, followed by a shot glass of horrible tasting oil, all on an empty stomach. In less than fifteen minutes, I had to run out of the seminar and throw up in the lobby of a nice hotel in Palm Springs. When I imagine that picture, I can see me running out of the room. The lights were dim. There was a terrible smell of wheatgrass vomit, plus the sound of retching. The image was low and to the left as I imagined it with my eyes closed.

Then, I went back to the happy picture of drinking coffee. I adjusted it to have all the same submodalities as the vomit picture. I made it darker. I pulled myself out of my body so I could see myself in the picture. I added the nasty smell and sounds to the movie. I moved the whole scene lower and to the left. Then I opened my eyes. I thought it was a joke. I didn't feel any different. Then the perfect cup of coffee appeared, just like I liked it. The man helping me through this process shoved the coffee right up under my nose and said, "You want some?" My body involuntarily recoiled, as if the coffee were a snake! As of the time I am writing this, I have not been near a cup of coffee in almost three years.

NOTE: This particular NLP process works great on memories that are *not* encoded with extremely painful negative emotions. If you have memories which carries a massive emotional charge, you need to use FasterEFT to release those strong emotions *before* using this simple technique. If your unconscious mind is hanging onto all that pain, it may not believe it is safe to change those internal references. Remember, the prime directive of the unconscious mind is to keep you safe. It will not allow you to do something that it believes will put you in danger. If you have severe traumatic references inside you, I highly recommend you hire a FasterEFT practitioner to release the big stuff. Go to www.FasterEFT.com/Practitioners to find a practitioner. The rest you can do on your own.

Your mind is interesting and powerful in ways you may never have imagined. As you practice the techniques in this book, I hope you will connect with me online and share your stories. The story of your success could save someone else's life.

STEP SIX EXERCISE

Exercise Your Imagination
Begin to play with your mind.
- Start with small habits and beliefs. Notice if, when you think about it, you have a picture. If you do, notice what the submodalities are. Write them down. If it is something you would like to get rid of, find a mental image of something similar that you hate and write down those submodalities. Then convert the thing you want to hate to have the submodalities of the thing you already hate and see what happens.

- Example: If you have a picture of something you dislike (like procrastination), imagine changing the quality of that image to one where you are excited and motivated. Begin to take charge of how your mind stores experiences, so you can change your behavior in the now and in the future.

STEP SEVEN

FORGIVE EVERYTHING AND EVERYONE

We don't forgive someone for their sake; we forgive them for the sake of our own peace of mind.... Do I put my faith in something loveless that someone did to me, or in the eternal love that lies beyond and corrects all things?

~Marianne Williamson

I hit a rough patch in my writing as I started this chapter. The previous six chapters flowed easily. But as I sat down to write about forgiveness, nothing came out. I put it off for several days, telling myself "It's the holidays. I'm traveling, visiting with family, and I just haven't had time." But even after I got home, I was still feeling very stuck.

I went back and read my previous chapters, and they reminded me that whatever is happening in my world is probably an expression of something inside me. I pushed through the resistance and tapped on not wanting to write until I let that go. Then I sat down at my computer and looked up the word 'forgive.' My online dictionary says the word forgive means to "Stop feeling angry or resentful toward someone for an offense, flaw or mistake."[9]

The first two words of that definition blew me away: "Stop feeling..."

---

[9] New Oxford American Dictionary (Second Edition) App for Mac OS X, Version 10.9.5.

Apparently, even the dictionary knows that forgiveness is not about what the other person did or did not do. Forgiveness is an inside job. Forgiveness changes how *you* feel about someone or something. Then it hit me. Who have I not forgiven? Who am I holding negative thoughts and emotions about inside me? Bingo! I have more work to do on my childhood, especially negative emotions I was holding about my mother. After about three hours of tapping and tears, I am now free of what was holding me back and I can now write this chapter.

What Is Forgiveness
If forgiveness is your ability to "Stop feeling angry or resentful toward someone for an offense, flaw or mistake", what does that mean? In real, tangible terms, it means that forgiveness involves changing your internal representations. That's it. What you hold in your mind about the things that have happened to you is what is controlling and hurting you.

Inside your mind, you have made a lifetime of decisions about what is good and what is bad; what is acceptable and what is shameful. You have made decisions about every person you have encountered, labeling them and their behaviors as good or bad, safe or dangerous, and choosing to be like them or different from them. All of your problems exist because of your perceptions, most of which you created before you had the knowledge or life experience to make a reasonable assessment of what was actually happening. That makes lack of forgiveness the number one cause of all problems. And here's why.

Two Models of the World
There are two models of the world; a Higher Model and a Lower Model. The Lower Model of the world is a child's model. The Higher Model of the world is one of personal responsibility.

When a child is born, it enters into a set of circumstances that simply exists. The child has parents or guardians who either love it, hate it, protect it, hurt it or ignore it. From the moment of birth, the child begins to encounter life and its new little empty brain is imprinted with every sight, sound, feeling, sensation, taste and emotion that it experiences. For each and every bit of information that comes in, the child will attach meaning to it. Humans are meaning making machines.

Two kids can grow up in the same house, with the same family and depending on their internal representation of it, they can describe two completely different childhoods. In my own family, my oldest brother would have a hard time saying anything nice about our mother while my youngest brother practically worshiped her. It is common for family circumstances to change and evolve over time. Parents can mellow or harden as they grow older. Two children, even ones close in age, can experience different worlds in the same household. But it is also possible for two children to create different meaning out of the same circumstances.

Celebrity brothers and authors, Frank and Malachy McCourt, both wrote memoirs about their childhood of extreme poverty and oppression in Ireland. Frank McCourt's award winning book *Angela's Ashes* is described as "somber and bleak," while Malachy McCourt's memoir *A Monk Swimming* is described as "a boisterous recollection fueled by his zestful appreciation for the opportunities and oddities of life." Same parents. Same home. Same school. Same lack of money and material things. Like the little optimist looking at all that horse manure, the quality of a person's life is greatly affected by how they internally process what happens to them and the meaning they give to it.

Lower Model of the World

In the beginning of life, all we can do is accept the world around us. We do not have any other information. It's all we know. So we simply receive input from our parents, babysitters, teachers, religious leaders, doctors, nurses, coaches, siblings, cousins, friends, aunts, uncles, strangers, police officers, movies, television, school, food, medicines, classes, animals, etc. Every experience from birth to early adulthood helps us to create what we believe to be true about the world. We learn things like: "Money doesn't grow on trees," "Doctor knows best," "Those people are bad," "You'll never amount to much," "You're fat," "People like us never get a break," "You have to work hard and then you die," "If I have a problem, a pill can solve it," "There is something wrong with me," "I'm not safe," and a billion other thoughts. On the other hand, some lucky children learn things like "You are beautiful and special," "You can always ask for help," and "No matter what happens, you can always find a solution." Unfortunately, I received and incorporated the first batch of beliefs.

When we are very young, we don't question anything because our brains are not equipped for that kind of processing. As I mentioned in Step One, a child's brain is operating at Theta until they are six or seven years old. This is equivalent to a hypnotic trance in an adult. Children simply accept what they see, hear, and feel as truth and then use those references to make decisions about the true nature of life. Our beliefs are based on the only information we have—our perceptions. This early education about the nature of our world is centered around 'They are doing it to me.' As a helpless, completely dependent little baby, there really is no alternative. Human babies rely on their mothers (and others) to feed and care for them for a longer period of time than any other living creature. Baby animals in the wild are often walking or swimming within minutes or even seconds after birth. But human babies are totally and completely dependent. So it is natural that humans often develop and hang onto the limiting perspective that 'They are doing it to me.'

If you are beaten, neglected, half starved, and told you are worthless and unwanted for the first eight years of life, you will have a much different perspective of the world than someone who was the greatly anticipated golden child, loved and given every opportunity to learn and grow and develop a high sense of self-esteem. But wishing your early life had been different will not alter your life. And neither will blaming your parents for where you are now. Your parents, relatives, teachers and friends could not give you what they did not have. They very likely did to you what someone else did to them. It is the way they learned how to do it. But right here, right now, you can choose to live from a higher model of the world.

Higher Model of the World

The Higher Model of the world is the exact opposite of the Lower Model. Instead of always assuming "They are doing it to me," you can take ownership of your life and recognize that inside your mind there are sights, sounds, sensations, smells, tastes and programs that run automatically. When something bothers you, instead of looking for the cause outside, you can look within for the mechanism that is being triggered and causing that feeling. And when you find it, you can change it and be free.

Once you learn how the mind works, you can begin to operate from the Higher Model of the world. You can change how you operate, even though you are still the same person who received the same input from your early environment.

In the last chapter, you learned how, as you experience life, you create a variety of internal references. All of these internal references have subtle qualities that give them meaning. The way to change what your memories mean is to change how you internally represent them. Let me explain how this works, because it is the secret to deep and lasting change.

When you close your eyes and imagine a picture, that image can be in color or black and white. It can be bright or dim, flat or 3D, a still or a movie, close or far away and in different locations around you. Sounds can be loud or soft, high or low, sweet or sinister and come from different directions. These are just a few of the many submodalities that can be tweaked.

When I use the word "feelings," I am talking about actual sensations in your body. If a client tells me they are angry, I ask "How do you know? Where do you feel it in your body?" Some will say anger is in their gut, others will say it is in their throat or chest. It may be a tightness or a heat or even a stone cold feeling. Anger is a skill. You must learn how to create it. Everyone does anger in their own way. The same is true for sadness, guilt, fear, disappointment and every other emotion. What most people don't realize is that their greatest power is in their emotions. Going to great lengths to escape those emotions works to cut you off from your power. Once you understand emotions and take control of them, they can begin to serve you instead of jerk you around.

In addition to submodalities, you also record and store *programs* (also known as trances) inside your mind. Programs are actions, feelings or thoughts you do or have automatically whenever they are triggered. If you are driving your car and a song comes on the radio that makes you sad, that song triggered a sadness program in your mind which runs an automatic response. Your mind has been programmed (or trained) to feel sad when it hears that song. The good news is, you can retrain your mind to produce a different feeling the next time you hear that song. You can also change your reaction to your boss's attitude, your x-husband's voice or mother-in-law's glare. And that can change your whole life.

As you become aware of how these internal representations are running your life, you can easily take ownership of them. Now, when you begin to have a problem, instead of blaming something out there and claiming "They are doing it to me," you can turn inward and say "Something inside me is making me feel angry" or depressed or any other emotion.

Using your new understanding and your new skill of FasterEFT, you can immediately address the emotion, uncover the program and release it. That is emotional intelligence and the way to step into your power. It's the fastest and easiest way to operate from the Higher Model of the world. It is also the secret to forgiving and releasing the pain you are carrying around inside you.

Escapaholism

We are all escapaholics on some level. We are all addicted to something that helps us escape from what bothers us. Whenever that thing happens that makes us feel uncomfortable, we run to our favorite coping mechanism. It could be food, drink, drugs, cigarettes, shopping, sex, cleaning, gambling or a hundred other things. But running from people, events or emotions will never solve anything. Wherever you go, your mind goes with you.

On top of that, escape mechanisms create additional problems. If you have a problem and you go outside for a smoke, when you come back, you still have your problem. If you eat a bag of chips and come back, your difficulty is still there. If you get drunk or high and come back later, you still have your predicament.

The problem with all these escape strategies is that they create *new* problems. Now, you have your original problem plus fifty extra pounds or cancer or a prison sentence. Escapism does not solve anything, it just creates more problems. The best thing you can do is take response-ability. Take control of your ability to respond by going within and addressing what bothers you. If it's just too painful, seek some help. Hire a FasterEFT practitioner. Yes, you do have to *go there* to that scary uncomfortable place you do not want to go, but only for a brief moment. Then you can release it and be free of it for the rest of your life. You do want to be free, happy and successful, don't you?

Ultimate Forgiveness

There have been many deep, serious philosophical and spiritual books written about forgiveness. My take on forgiveness is simple. I believe forgiveness is a matter of emotional intelligence. It involves recognizing that you are hurting you now. At some point in the past, yes, someone else did this painful thing to you. But the best part about the past is that the past is over. Recognize that *now*, you are doing that thing to you, inside your mind.

This is not an excuse to blame, shame or beat yourself up. In fact, it is exactly the opposite. When you begin to function from the Higher Model of the world by taking one hundred percent responsibility for how you feel, you take back your power. You are no longer a victim to anyone, including yourself!

Learning a new skill that allows you to release all the hurts and all the painful memories will free you from the pain and bondage of unforgiveness. You do not have to condone anyone's bad behavior to release your pain. What they did is not your concern. There is a Law of Cause and Effect operating in the Universe. Everyone will eventually experience the effects of their actions. When and how that happens is not your concern. The only thing you can control is what is going on inside you now. Recognizing that you are carrying around unnecessary pain, fear and grief and giving yourself the gift of letting it go is the highest form of loving yourself, forgiving yourself and loving the world.

Hurt people, hurt people. Bullies are usually operating out of their own pain and insecurity. A policy of "Never Forget" is giving unconscious permission for it to happen again. The quickest way to world peace is for each and every person on Earth to release the hurts they hold inside. As long as you are hurting yourself inside your own mind, you will continue to hurt yourself and others. When you learn to change how you represent your past and let go of the pain, that is Ultimate Forgiveness.

STEP SEVEN EXERCISES

Forgiveness Opportunities
Search your Peace List for forgiveness opportunities.
- Make a list of people you need to forgive for whatever reason.

- Make a list of things you need to forgive yourself for doing or not doing.

- Tap until you are free. It was never about them anyway.

- Write an entry in your Happy Journal describing what it feels like to forgive and be free.

- Make a list of all the wonderful people who have touched your life in some way. Add that list to your Happy Journal.

STEP EIGHT

CREATE A MEANINGFUL RELATIONSHIP WITH YOURSELF

*Religion is a belief in someone else's experience.
Spirituality is having your own experience.*

~Deepak Chopra

I used to agonize about not having a meaningful enough relationship with my parents, certain family members, and on occasion, even with my husband. But then a friend gave me a big insight by asking me "Who do you spend the most time with, other people or yourself?" It never occurred to me that I should think about having a meaningful relationship with myself. If I had to be handcuffed to another person for the rest of my life, I would really want it to be someone I had a great relationship with, wouldn't you?

Wherever you go, you take yourself with you. So isn't it time to give this idea some space in your brain? But where do you start?

Put Yourself First

Most of us were taught at a young age that it is selfish to put ourselves first. There are a lot of misunderstandings around what is selfish and what is putting yourself first. Selfishness is defined as "lacking consideration for others; concerned chiefly with one's own personal profit and pleasure."[10] Focusing solely on personal profit and pleasure is not putting your true self first. Putting yourself first means to devote care and consideration to your physical, mental and spiritual well-being. You cannot give what you do not have. If you do not love and care for yourself, how can you love and care for someone else?

A mother in India once brought her young diabetic son to visit Mahatma Gandhi. She wanted Gandhi, this man they both regarded as holy and wise, to tell her son to stop eating sugar. She trusted that her son would listen to Gandhi and do what he said. After hearing the woman's plea, he refused to talk to the boy and requested that she bring him back in two weeks. The woman complained that the journey had been long and hard, but Gandhi insisted she go home and return in two weeks. With great time, effort, and expense, she did as she was told. Two weeks later, she brought her son back to see Gandhi and Gandhi told the boy to stop eating sugar. The woman was grateful, and politely asked why he made her wait. Gandhi replied that he could not tell the boy to stop eating sugar while he was still eating it.

As a FasterEFT practitioner, I often tap on myself prior to a session with a client. I look for their issues in me and tap away any similar internal programs before I see them. When I am completely free of whatever is controlling or limiting my client, then I am able to facilitate better results for my client. By creating proof in myself that their problem has no real power, I am empowered to help them do the same. By putting myself first, I am able to give much more to others. And, as an added benefit, I heal myself.

Putting yourself first means loving yourself. You cannot love anyone else until you love yourself. Selfishness comes from too little self-love, not too much. People who are always looking to get something from others are exhibiting a deep seated feeling of lack. Selfish people may appear to be helping themselves, but they are usually hurting themselves in the process.

Selfish people are never really kind to themselves. Their inner dialog is harsh and judgmental and nothing is ever enough. They are self-centered because they believe there is something intrinsically wrong

---

10 New Oxford American Dictionary (Second Edition) App for Mac OS X, Version 10.9.5.

with them, and they have to fix it with something outside themselves at any cost.

I know this because I have been there. As a child, I felt completely inadequate. Nothing I could do or say was ever right or enough. And I have spent a lifetime trying every self-help book, seminar, and healing modality to eliminate that empty feeling inside me.

The mind expresses itself in metaphors. Recently, I was tapping on an issue with a certain food I was craving when the image of an unfillable black hole popped into my head. Using FasterEFT, I tapped away the metaphor that my mind was producing and, as a result, dissolved the uncomfortable feeling of never having enough.

If you have ever had a feeling deep inside that you are not enough, then you know the constant drive to fill that emptiness with things, experiences, money or achievements. You fill it with food, drugs, drinks, sex, fighting or some other distraction. There is no substance, trophy or experience that can make you feel that you are enough inside you. That constant outward neediness creates a destructive downward spiral. Trying to fill an inner void with outward things is backwards thinking and it will never get you to a happy or peaceful place. It's wonderful to have things you want. But wanting them and being desperate for them are two completely different experiences.

People who learn to change their thinking and truly put their physical, mental and spiritual health first are often the most giving, selfless people you have ever met. That is because they are operating from wholeness. They are so filled with love and acceptance that there is no need for competition, jealousy or hatred.

When you take the time and make the effort to go within and clean up your thoughts and beliefs, then you begin to recognize your true value, which automatically creates a loving attitude towards yourself and your world.

When you love yourself, you are in integrity. You are complete, whole, and lacking nothing. When you operate from integrity, then your desires can serve both you and your world in beautiful ways. Desire becomes your contribution to life. Your unique desires are the Universe expanding with newness—as you.

When you are full of love and valuing your own life, then you can love and value others. Your desires will then bring you joy and fulfillment. When you are radiating those qualities, your world will benefit from you expressing your unique desire. Jane Goodall once said, "You do not have to save the whole world. Find your piece of the puzzle." Your actions and your love will become contagious.

If the thought of putting yourself first feels bad or wrong to you, recognize you are running a mental program. Along the road of life, you learned that concept of selfishness from someone important to you. And they learned it from someone in their past. A program is just a learned behavior. Deal with it now. Tap to change it. You are the boss of you, whether you acknowledge it or not. Own your power. Address your emotions, memories and thoughts and free yourself. If you do not love and care for you, no one else can.

The World Is Your Mirror

Feeling empty and worthless creates self-loathing. When you hate yourself, you only see what you hate in other people, places, things and situations you encounter. Maybe not at first, but eventually. That new car looks good when you buy it. And for a while, you feel good in it. But after a few months or a year, that car becomes routine and it no longer makes you feel as good as it once did. The same thing can happen with relationships. At first, you are giddy and excited. The new attention makes you feel lovable and special. But if you do not already love yourself, when the newness wears off, you will begin to see the not-enoughness reflected back to you in their eyes. And you will blame them for becoming not enough when the problem was inside you all along.

How you perceive your world is a reflection of your relationship with yourself. Your relationship with your addiction is a mirror of your relationship with yourself. Some people have a hard time with that idea because they have spent their entire life looking at what happens to them as coming from outside and being either good or bad. It is either an angel helping or the devil punishing. The truth is, it is neither of those things. The world gives you feedback. Based on your perceptions and beliefs, you then assign meaning to what happens. Even if you see something horrible on the news that happened half way around the world, how you respond to it is a reflection of what is going on inside you at some level. You can feel angry, sad, or terrified for those people and suffer with them, which does not help them one bit. You only hurt yourself (and probably everyone around you.) There are other options. You can look at bad news as a call to prayer. Or you can start a movement to send aid, people and supplies. Or you could find where something similar is going on in your own community and find or create a way to help there.

Sometimes, you need to turn off the world and focus on your own health and well-being, at least for a while. Because if you are not healthy, there is not much you can do for others. Learning how to have a healthy emotional response makes you far more capable of helping those in need, including yourself.

Enemy Or Friend?

Albert Einstein said: "I think the most important question facing humanity is, 'Is the Universe a friendly place?' This is the first and most basic question all people must answer for themselves." Einstein further described the ramifications of how you choose to answer that question for yourself.

If you decide that the world is not a friendly place, then you will use all of your resources and creativity to either fight or avoid everything and everyone that you imagine as unfriendly. If you decide that the world is neither friendly nor unfriendly and that God is playing dice with the Universe, then you will become a victim to the random toss of the dice and your life will have no purpose or meaning. But if you decide that the world is a friendly place, then you will use all your resources to create understanding and new solutions. Power automatically comes to you through creativity and joy.

The world is your friend. Everything that happens to you and around you is your best friend telling you what you need to work on next. By taking responsibility for how you feel and living from the higher model of the world, you will begin to see everything that happens as a gift. It is the gift of feedback. You will stop taking everything personally. You will stop operating from the perspective of "They're doing it to me" and you will begin to function from the perspective of "I am doing something inside me that is making me feel this way." Only then will you be truly in control of your life. Only then will you stand in your power. Only then will you be operating from cause, not effect.

People's words and actions represent what they hold within them. When you squeeze a lemon, you get lemon juice, not orange juice or pear juice. Lemon juice is just what is inside. It's all the lemon has. When things happen and your world begins to put the squeeze on you, your reaction depends entirely on what you are holding within. If you do not like your results, the only real and lasting way to change them is to go within and deal with the real cause.

Use your mirror—your world—as your guide. Make those uncomfortable circumstances your best friend, instead of your enemy. Notice what you do not like and go after the real cause within. Once you clean up the cause, you will never have to suffer those negative effects again. You will have peace inside you, and that peace will begin showing up in your world, because the world is your mirror. As you develop a better relationship with yourself, you will improve your relationship with everything and everyone else.

How Do You Talk To Yourself?

Remember the exercise in Step Three where you spoke statements and wrote down your internal response? Those responses clearly illustrated how you talk to yourself. How did those responses make you feel? Would you let anyone else talk to you like that? I think not! So why do you put up with it *from you*? Because you have never been trained to question what goes on inside your own head. You accept your internal dialogue as truth, without question, just like you accepted the dialogue of your caregivers when you were a baby. But you are all grown up now. So, don't believe everything you think! People slip into patterns of thought in the same way they slip into patterns of action or inaction. Find a way to break your pattern of negative thinking.

Breaking Your Pattern

I belong to Toastmasters where I have a lot of fun honing my public speaking skills. At every meeting, one person is designated the "Ah" counter. Near the end of the meeting, this person stands up and tells everyone how many "ahs" and "ums" they had. One week, I visited a different club. Instead of counting the "ahs" and "ums", they had a bell. If you said "ah" or "um" right in the middle of your speech, you received a loud DING! It shocked my system. And it was a great *pattern interrupt*. In the meetings where I heard the count— "Marguerite, you had six ahs and two ums"—it created an *awareness* about what I needed to work on, but just hearing about it intellectually never helped me stop doing it. It just aggravated me that I had this problem. The bell was another story. It was like using an electric shock to change behavior.

The bell makes a loud noise in the present moment, interrupting the behavior as it is happening. Interruption is a powerful strategy to use with your thoughts.

If something comes to mind that you recognize as an old pattern, immediately stop and tell your negative thought to "Shut up!" Feel free to use stronger language, if you prefer. "Shut the #&@% up!" (Fill in your favorite curse word.)

Back in the 1970s, Louise Hay started a popular trend of saying "Cancel, cancel" whenever you say or think something negative. You can also tap on wherever that negative thought or belief came from and let it go. Whatever you do, once you have told it to go away, be sure to create a positive replacement. If you have said "I can't remember where I put my keys", say "Stop that! I have a perfect mind with perfect recall."

If you think this kind of self-talk is weird, just go back and look at the rubbish your mind was saying to you before you decided to take control. Trust me, this is way less weird and a whole lot more helpful.

Know What You Want

Occasionally, people become stuck in their strong intention to change what they do not want. Letting go of what you do not want is definitely the place to start. You would not walk into a house that had been abandoned for ten years and immediately start decorating it, would you? No, you would do some cleaning and maybe even a little restructuring first. The same is true for your mind. Besides, do you even know what you *really* want?

So many people live their life as if their hair is on fire, running around trying to fix one disaster after another. They are so busy putting out fires that they don't have time to even contemplate what would make them happy. Have you ever felt that way? Or known someone who lives that way?

Having a meaningful relationship with someone implies that you know them at a deep level. Knowing someone deeply means you are aware of their goals and dreams. If you have not discussed your goals and dreams with the people closest to you, it is a safe bet that you have not spent much time thinking about them either, at least not for a long time.

Statistics say that ninety percent of people do not create and write down any type of goals or desires. They are simply not having that conversation with themselves.

I am not talking about wishing or hoping. Wishing and hoping both imply there is a strong likelihood it is not going to happen. Wishing for a smaller waist line or hoping for a promotion can be downright destructive to your self-esteem. Wishing and hoping your problem will go away could even be killing you. Focusing your energy on wishing and hoping is setting yourself up for failure. Wishing and hoping come from fear and a feeling of helplessness, hopelessness and not having any control.

On top of that, people rarely wish for what they truly want. They tend to wish for what they *think* they should have. Most people do not even know who or what they want to be. Ask a five year old what she wants to be and she will say something like "I want to be a doctor, a singer and a princess!" No limits. Then, she learns to shut that down and do what pleases the adults around her. Suddenly, we are all grown up and still operating from that little girl or little boy that just wanted to be loved and accepted.

I have secretly always been a little jealous of people who knew what they wanted to be at a very young age. You hear a lot of those stories during the Olympics. How does the ice dancer or hockey player know they want to be an athlete at the age of four? Are they just lucky? Or did they have people around them who encouraged and supported their choices? And what if you are thirty-five or fifty-three or even eighty and you want to start over? How do you figure out what you really want?

If you sit down and write out a list of what you want, I can almost guarantee it will not be what you *really* want. It will be a list of what you think you should have or what you can have without upsetting your relatives and friends. The only way to discover the heart of what you truly want in life is to go in and clear away what you *do not want* first. What you do not want drives your entire life. The most powerful motivators are those things that you do not want.

People will go to crazy extremes to avoid what they do not want. We busy ourselves and waste massive amounts of time all in the service of avoiding what we do not want. We spend so much time thinking about and avoiding what we do not want that we never have time to discover what we truly want. The more pain a person is carrying around, the more likely they are to become an escape-aholic.

An interesting thing happens when you go within and transform your painful memories. New visions of possibility and opportunity begin to appear. Things that never occurred to you before, suddenly become possible and exciting.

Back when I was stuck in my pattern of thinking that the world was not a friendly place, the thought of wanting to be a public speaker never even crossed my mind. It was simply not an option for someone who was afraid of everyone and everything. I never worked on my fear of public speaking because it never occurred to me to do so. I did not want to do anything that would put me in an unsafe place, like on a stage in front of a room full of people all looking at me! But after I turned within and released my old memories of being bullied, I literally woke up one day and thought, "Hey, I'd like to be a public speaker."

This is what I want you to understand. When you change what you hold within, your whole world changes. *Automatically.*

There has never been a more potent example of this than Mahatma Gandhi. When he was growing up, he and almost a billion of his fellow countrymen felt the tyranny and oppression of British rule. Did they have good reasons to feel oppressed? Absolutely! It was a repressive and often cruel regime. The population responded in one of three ways. A few decided to fight against their oppressors, which usually ended badly. Some retreated to remote areas or tried to hide from authorities. But most felt hopeless to change their situation and gave in to the oppression in order to survive. All three of these solutions focus on what is going on outside. They were operating from the Lower Model of the world where 'They are doing it to me.'

Most people could see no other option. But one man decided to do something revolutionary. He decided to turn within and change the contents of his own mind, which put him in contact with previously unimagined resources. With his new approach, Gandhi changed not just his own life, but his entire country. And in doing so, he created a ripple effect that spread across the entire world. The largest and most powerful empire in the world at that time was no match for this one little man in a loin cloth who decided to tap into the power of his own mind. His mind was not special. It was no different from yours. The only difference is that he decided to form a relationship with his mind and to use it fully.

You have no idea what you are capable of until you go inside your mind and create a new relationship with yourself. This is what Gandhi did. And I believe it is what Jesus meant when he said "Turn the other cheek." I don't believe he meant you should allow someone to slap you some more. I believe he was telling us to turn our heads and look in a different direction, away from outside circumstances. Turn away from the outward pain and suffering and turn inward, because that is where your power lies. And, that is where God is.

STEP EIGHT EXERCISES

Peace List
Continue writing and tapping on your Peace List.
- If you have a traditional Fourth Step Inventory, turn it into your Peace List.

- Tap on each memory until you create peace where there used to be pain.

- AFTER you clear the negative emotions out of each memory, ask yourself, what you would rather have experienced in that moment? Journal about the joyful, peaceful, loving experience you would rather have had. Make it up. Make it as beautiful as you can. Imagine it fully and feel all the good feelings in your body as you do.

- Begin to practice your new, made up memory as if it was real. (Remember, you must clear out all negative emotions first or this will be difficult.)

Happy Journal
Spend time reading your Happy Journal and continue to add to it. Go make some new happy memories and write them in your Happy Journal. Don't wait for them to happen. Make them happen!

STEP NINE

BECOME NON-JUDGMENTAL

*The problem of good and evil will never enter the mind
which is at peace within itself.*

~Ernest Holmes

One of the wonderful consequences of releasing my painful past and tapping away everything that starts to bother me is that I am naturally becoming less and less judgmental, both towards myself and others. When I operate from one hundred percent response-ability for how I feel, I begin to realize that judgment is not a logical place to invest my time and energy. The truest understanding I have about reality is embodied in the Law of Cause and Effect.

The Law of Cause and Effect
The Law of Cause and Effect states that for every cause, there is an effect and for every effect, there is a cause. Every action produces a consequence which you will ultimately have to experience. No one escapes this law, even though it may appear that some do. Eventually, you will reap what you sow. Your punishment may come in a form that outsiders cannot see, but it will happen. Every time. You have no idea what goes on inside the mind of someone who does horrible things or inside the mind of a person who does not love themselves. The ravages

of cancer and many other diseases have been directly linked to stress and negative emotions. There are a million ways to pay for your choices.

Identifying the true cause of your problems can become confusing. So many people blame their circumstances for all their problems. But what caused the circumstances? I am not suggesting that you transfer the blame and shame from outside of you to inside of you. Sometimes, life just happens. Maybe you were born into a terrible situation or you became friends with the crowd where bad things happened all the time. Your power is not in judging the situation to be bad or good. Your power is in your ability to simply acknowledge where you are and then do something about your response to what is happening.

"Actions drive results." We have all heard that phrase from every motivational guru on the planet. But what drives action? Most of those gurus will tell you that it is just a decision you make. Get with the program! But the driver of action is always mental, and often it is a deeply held belief or program that you are not even aware of. The content of your subconscious mind—your beliefs, attitudes, motives, thoughts, desires and programs—determine your actions. That is why New Year's resolutions almost never last more than a week or two. On the surface, we say we want to lose weight or quit drinking, but if there is a program or belief in the subconscious mind that says "If you are thin, you will be disliked, or worse, attacked", or "If you are sober, you'll lose your best friend," then your actions will be sabotaged.

The Saboteur Within

Do we really sabotage ourselves? I used to get so upset with myself for not being able to keep a promise I made to myself. I would have big ideas and make plans for the future that would be scrapped inside a week. Sometimes they didn't last a whole day! I felt so helpless and weak and worthless. I just knew there had to be something inside me that was evil—a gremlin or a saboteur that had it in for me. I wanted to figure out what that was and conquer it, vanquish it, basically kill it. I was at war with myself.

I judged my own mind, assuming the worst, that there was something terrible inside me that I had to fight. And since I did not know any better, I began to operate from that erroneous idea. I began to hate myself for being so weak. My self-talk became more and more negative, and when I spoke to others, I was very self-deprecating, always throwing myself under the bus. If anyone gave me a compliment, I had a snappy comeback that destroyed it. Why did I do that? Was it the 'saboteur within?'

There is no saboteur within. The prime directive of the unconscious mind is to keep you safe. Everything you do and say expresses what is deeply buried in your subconscious mind. Those seemingly crazy things you do are not something inside you that is trying to hurt you. *It is actually your subconscious mind trying to keep you safe.*

Somewhere in your past experience, your subconscious mind learned that it is not safe or not okay to have, be or do certain things. If your parents, relatives and friends were all talking trash about rich people, saying they must have done something bad to attain all that money, or they must be mean, horrible people, your unconscious mind will create amazing roadblocks and difficulties to keep you from ever becoming rich. If you do manage to make money, your unconscious mind will create clever ways for you to spend it or lose it.

Your mind is not a saboteur. Your mind is acting out of great love and concern for you. Your unconscious mind uses the only resources it has, the ones that were installed by powerful first impressions, loaded with emotional content. If you want to change your current results, in any area of your life, you must change the cause behind it. And if that is true for you, it is also true for everyone you encounter.

Judging Others

Whatever someone says or does to you is what they are thinking about themselves. Let me say that again, because it is really important. Everything that comes out of another person's mouth is really about *them*. It has nothing to do with you. When you squeeze a lemon, you get lemon juice because that is what is inside. The only thing a person can give you is what they have inside. If hate, jealousy, shame, or any other emotion overwhelms their interior landscape, that same emotion will eventually leach out onto other people. Your best response is to remember that hurt people, hurt people. Everything they say expresses some aspect of what they feel about themselves, not you. To judge them and make up a story about them is flawed thinking. If you witness someone doing something hurtful, remember, they are operating from a trance; a pattern; a program. You can choose to have it stop with you by changing your reaction, rather than trying to change them.

There is a famous quote from Chief Red Eagle, "Angry people want you to see how powerful they are. Loving people want you to see how powerful you are." People who feel powerless inside will try to make themselves feel powerful by making others feel powerless. It is a program. And, if you are encountering such a program in your experience, take responsibility for your response by making the effort to clear whatever it is inside you that their behavior triggered.

Their behavior may look very different from how you do the same emotion, but there is some aspect of what is happening to you (as an adult) that is buried in your subconscious mind.

If you were abused as a child, it is very important to go within and make peace with your past. When you clear it completely, you will no longer encounter people like that. Or if you do, it will be at a distance, and it will not upset you in the way it used to. You will feel a different emotion. Perhaps compassion. Or, you may be inspired to take some constructive action to help others who are suffering.

Some people judge without provocation. They have a strong program that considers evaluating and naming things in a negative light a means for keeping them separate and therefore safe. Have you ever known anyone like that? I remember having lunch with a woman at an outdoor cafe when a very overweight man walked by on the street. This woman immediately started making negative, judgmental comments about the man, out loud. I wanted to crawl under the table and hide! I asked her why she did that and she said "They need to know that's not okay and they should do something about it." I later learned that when she was a child, criticism and judgment was doled out like others give pep talks. She and I had very different ideas about what constitutes compassion. But all she knew was what she had been taught by her family.

What she failed to understand is that judgmental thoughts and words eventually operate against the person who speaks them. I know for a fact that this woman often felt the sting of harsh judgment and rejection in many areas of her own life. She also developed severe health issues, including several battles with cancer. No one can be happy when they live in a constant state of condemning people, conditions or things. It is time we learn how to praise more and condemn less. And not just each other. It is time we all learned to praise and appreciate ourselves.

Judging Yourself

No one judges or condemns us like we judge and condemn ourselves. What some people call sins, I call mistakes. In fact, the Classical Greek word that translates as 'sin' actually meant 'to miss the mark.' The root of the English word 'sin' also comes from an Old English archery term. If the archer missed the bull's eye, it was a 'sin.' Our sins are our mistakes, places where we missed the mark. They are the thoughts and actions that come from ignorance or unconscious programs.

We only know what we know and then we act on those learned ideas. Later in life, we may hear information that contradicts what we learned as a child, but our unconscious mind is more attached to the information that was programmed in with those emotionally charged early experiences. Unless you can interrupt that old pattern of thinking with something stronger, the old pattern will override logic every time. Your power is in your emotions. Using the emotional intelligence that comes from practicing FasterEFT tapping, you can make peace with old negative emotions and behaviors, and then install new positive ones.

As you travel through life making mistakes, you end up suffering the consequences of those mistakes. Some would call that punishment. I call it results or effects. The Law of Cause and Effect operates perfectly. When you feel like you are being punished, it helps to look for the true cause. The real cause is a mistake in thinking. When you correct and forgive the mistake, you no longer suffer from it.

To judge yourself is to limit yourself. Instead of judging and condemning yourself, learn to love and praise yourself. Maybe you didn't have anyone in your childhood who knew how to love themselves, so you had no one to teach you those skills. But it's never too late to learn. Ultimately, the only thing that judges us is the Law of Cause and Effect. You are your own reward, and you are your own punishment.

STEP NINE EXERCISES

Mirror Exercise
This is a popular exercise, but it only works if you actually do it!

- Stand in front of a mirror. Look into your own eyes and say to yourself, with feeling, "I love you." If any resistance comes up in the form of inner dialog or negative feelings, tap it away.

- Repeat the exercise until you can say "I love you" while looking into your own eyes and feeling a good sensation inside.

- Commit to doing this every day for 90 days. Journal about your experience. If you do this exercise, it will have a profound effect on your life.

STEP TEN

LIVE FROM NON-ATTACHMENT

When I let go of what I am, I become what I might be.
When I let go of what I have, I receive what I need.

~Tao Te Ching

We all like to have stuff. And it's natural to want more of what makes you happy, whatever that is. For some, it may be a new car or jewelry, for others it's a child or a romantic relationship. I am not here to judge what anyone wants. Whatever it is for you, I believe you should have it. The things we want are not the problem. Problems appear when we fall down and worship the things we want. When we do that, we give all our power away to those things.

The only reason anyone desires anything is because of how they *believe* it will make them *feel*. There is no other reason to want anything. Ultimately, your power resides in your emotions. Why not go straight to the source and simply change how you feel?

When we place inappropriate significance on what we desire, or even the things we already have, then what we desire becomes an obsession. What we want to possess begins to possess us. What we want to control, controls us.

There is one quote from the Bible that I believe is misquoted more often than any other. How many times have I seen someone look down their nose at a successful, happy person and say "Money is the root of all evil?" I have compassion for that person because their perspective will never allow them to be a financial success. Someone close to them believed that money was evil, and they passed their program on with strong emotion, backed by proof—what they were told was a quote from the Bible.

The good news is, that is not what the Bible says. The actual quote is "The *love of* money is the root of all evil." And the word "love" in this instance is an unfortunate translation. A better translation would be "The worship of money is the root of all evil." Money, in and of itself, is nothing. It is neither good nor bad. It just is. The world used to operate on the barter system, but that became very cumbersome. You can't very easily bring your old couch to the grocery to exchange for food. So money was invented as a more convenient form of exchange. Money is something humans have decided has value, but that value changes every day. Anyone can open an account and begin trading on the Forex Exchange. You can watch the value of dollars, Pounds, Euros, Yen, and Pesos go up and down all day long. None of it has any meaning except the meaning you give it.

And it's not just money. Whenever you put anything on a pedestal and worship it as if it has more value than life or love or joy, then you become a slave to that thing. When you recognize that money is useful and has its place as a tool in a modern society, then you can use it to create all manner of goodness in the world. You can provide shelter, safety, health, warm clothes, and joyful experiences to yourself and others. Your desire is never about the thing itself. It's never about the money, the shoes, the house, the ring, or even the husband, wife or baby. You are limiting yourself by thinking you must have certain things to feel good. There are millions of ways to feel good right now, right where you are. And the more you practice feeling good, the more good things will begin to appear in your experience. It really is all about how you feel, right here, right now.

Attachment As Love

Never confuse attachment with love. Attachment is a function of fear and dependency. When you are attached to anything, an object, a person, an idea or an outcome, it is because you are afraid of losing it. And you are afraid of losing it because you are afraid of how losing it will make you feel.

Nothing in life is permanent. There is an ebb and flow to life just as there is an ebb and flow to all the things and people that populate our existence. They come and go freely. Clamping down on something and trying to hold it still never works for very long. Life is always moving. Water must flow. Flowers bloom and die. Everything is cyclical. A healthy lake has an ingress where water feeds into it as well as an egress where water flows out. It may look like a still, unmoving, self-contained body of water, but it never is. When we dam things up, that causes problems. Stagnant water eventually begins to grow weird things and have a nasty smell. You cannot live by only inhaling. You must constantly inhale and exhale. In and out. Ebb and flow.

Life brings us new experiences every moment of every day. There is always information coming in, and your brain makes note of all those incoming signals. The brain creates meaning for them and stores them in the great reference library called your mind. This storehouse of information creates the map of what you believe to be true about your world. The only way to change what is true about your world is to change the information storehouse that creates your map of what you believe is true. FasterEFT is one way to transform that storehouse of information and open the mind to new possibilities.

When you release your attachment to things and ideas, you are free to be present with what is, in the moment. Attachment is neither good nor bad. It's a process. Attachment tends to take us away from the present moment. It either puts us into fear, thanks to a painful memory from the past where we did not have what we needed or wanted, or it puts us into the future, worrying about losing something or not ever having it. You can never love a person while you are worried about losing them. You are either spending time loving and enjoying your baby, or you are suffering as you look at this baby and imagine losing it. You cannot do both at the same time.

For your sake, and for the sake of others in your experience, be present! Release your attachment to anything other than what you really want to be feeling right now. *Make how you feel right now your priority.* Focus your mind on the positive. That does not mean you stop paying your bills and bliss out on chocolate cake. It means, whatever you do, do it mindfully. As you pay your bills, recognize how amazing it is that someone trusts you enough to give you what you want right away and let you pay them later. How awesome is that?! Bless them. Thank your electric company for the heat or air conditioning you enjoyed before you ever gave them a dime. Be present with your baby or your lover or your work. And when you switch to something else, be present with that. Living from Non-Attachment is one of the greatest gifts you can give yourself. It is the secret to real freedom and authentic choice. As you clear out more and more of your old unconscious patterns, you will begin to notice that you automatically begin to live from less and less attachment. You may also notice that you begin to enjoy what you do have more and more.

Being Right

One of the strongest and most destructive attachments I have come across is in people who are attached to being right. The need to be right is not uncommon, but it seems to be especially activated in the world now. The need to be right brings healthy political discourse to a standstill. No one seems to be discussing the important issues of the day anymore. The currently popular behavior choice looks more like digging ruts on both sides of an issue and lobbing verbal bombs back and forth. The only difference between a rut and a grave is that a rut has no ends.

Everyone has a right to their opinion and their choice of belief and lifestyle. And for those of us who live in a place that values freedom and expression—we are lucky! But with freedom comes responsibility. There's that word again. Response-Ability. The one thing that you have absolute control over is your mind. And because you control your thoughts, you control your response to everything that happens around you. Your ability to control how you respond to your environment in every moment will determine the quality of your life. You get to choose.

Do you want to be right or do you want to be happy? Some people think that being right will make them happy. But in my experience, it usually just makes you lonely and bitter. Think about someone you know who always has to be right. Go ahead. Think of someone. How happy do you think they really are? How's their health? Their marriage? Their bank account? Just when you think someone you idolize is so perfect—they are rich, successful, respected, and maybe even famous. Then, you find out they are addicted to prescription pain medication or have some stress-related disease. Do you still think being right makes you happy? What's really going on inside their mind? Obviously, more than appearances would suggest.

Releasing Old Attachments

This is where people start to grow uncomfortable with me. They think I am going to take away their favorite coping mechanism. And then how will they handle those unwanted emotions? I never take anything away from anyone. It's not even possible. Oh, I could (with some help) tie you up or imprison you to keep you away from your stuff for a while, but as soon as you are released, if nothing inside you has changed, you'll go right back to it. Just taking away someone's coping mechanism is cruel because it causes pain. Working on the effect without addressing the underlying cause of the problem is also wasted effort. The only sure way to release your attachment to an old response is to give you the ability to respond differently. And the only way to respond differently is to change what you hold within.

Happiness and choice are possible when you learn how to take control of how you represent things internally. By changing the pictures, sounds, feelings and programs in your subconscious mind, you will naturally and automatically release your attachment to your problem. When you let go of those old memory attachments, you create peace inside you. And when you have peace within, your whole world will be transformed before your eyes. Only then can you begin to address and release the old coping mechanisms.

STEP TEN EXERCISES

Notice Your Attachments

Practice noticing what you are attached to. (I am not talking about basic things like food, water and shelter.)

- Start small. Are you attached to an article of clothing or a piece of jewelry? Or maybe even a particular brand of diet soft drink or a television show? It may also be something you really want and don't have, like a job or winning the lottery. Journal about all the feelings that make you want it or what makes you feel like you can't be happy without it. Make sure you include how you feel (or would feel) when you do have it and how it would make you feel to not have it. You may notice that your life and death probably does not depend on the item itself. The important aspect is how that thing makes you feel.

- Practice feeling the feeling you thought that thing would give you. There are a million ways to make yourself feel the way that thing would make you feel. It's a choice. When you take back your power and direct your mind and body to feel a certain way, things that match that feeling will begin to show up in your life. God, the Universe, or whatever name you want to give it, often has a way of giving you something that makes you feel even better than the thing you were attached to receiving.

STEP ELEVEN

CREATE WITH INTENTIOIN

*"When the intention is clear, the mechanism will appear.
If how to's were enough, we'd all be skinny, rich and happy."*

~Brian Klemmer

When I was twenty-three years old, I wanted to live and study in England. I worked very hard for two years to gain entrance into the prestigious program called *The Works of Art Course* given by Sotheby's auction house in London. There was only one problem. I couldn't afford it. My mother managed to scrape up the funds to cover tuition, but I had no way of paying for food and a place to live in one of the most expensive cities in the world. Somehow, I managed to spend exactly zero time thinking about this problem. My thoughts were completely focused on going. I had absolutely no idea how it was going to happen, I just knew in every fiber of my being that I was going. My intention was crystal clear. I bought a nice warm coat and a radio that operated on both American and European electrical current. I had no idea how, I just trusted that somehow, some way, this was happening. About a month before the program was scheduled to start, a cousin I barely knew at the time flew into my home town and asked my mother to lunch. Knowing that this cousin lived in London, Mama took me along. Over lunch, my cousin asked if I would like to live with her while I was studying in London. She ended up paying most of my expenses for over a year, and we became fast friends. Was it a miracle? I can't say for sure. All I know is I have never had a stronger or more clear intention in my whole life.

One of the most important things to remember is, you are always creating something. Whatever cause you have set into motion will produce some kind of effect. The question to ask yourself is, are you getting the results you want?

We humans have this wonderful thing called free will. We have the ability to choose, in every moment, joy or sadness, fear or compassion, love or anger. Life is an ever-expanding, constantly creating energy and intelligence. That energy and intelligence expresses itself through thought. Only you can choose your thoughts. Eventually, your thoughts become things. Everything that has ever been created started out as a thought. So, the easiest and most effective way to change things is to start by changing your thoughts.

Unfortunately, most of us were not taught this principle as children. The only thing our parents could teach us is what they knew how to do. So we very often end up adopting their coping mechanisms as well as their ability to create problems. Is it any wonder that we end up wandering through life like we're in a boat without a rudder? We get tossed around by random storms and current events, believing that we are a victim to whatever life throws at us. Most people die without ever realizing that their rudder was inside them all the time. That rudder is your intention.

What Is Intention?

The dictionary defines intention as "a plan that one has in mind, or a determination to act in a certain way."[11] An intention is not a goal. A goal is the *object* of a person's intention. It is the desired end result. Goals are often things, numbers or outcomes. Intention plays a very different role. Intention is the mental and emotional fuel that drives your action and your choices.

Most of us operate from a default setting. Our brains uploaded the beliefs prevalent in our childhood environment, and then we operate as if those beliefs are absolutely true. Beliefs like "Money is hard to

---

11 New Oxford American Dictionary (Second Edition) App for Mac OS X, Version 10.9.5.

come by" or "No one will ever love me." It can be frustrating when our reality says "Money is hard to get" and someone comes into our life who believes "Money is easy." We can become very upset with people whose belief system is completely different from ours. We make up terrible stories about them. "How dare they come around here with all their dirty money!" Why do we do that? We make up stories about people who are different because our unconscious mind will do *anything* to substantiate our existing beliefs, even if it hurts.

The underlying intention of your unconscious mind is to keep you safe, and if your experience of the world does not line up with your beliefs, it causes chaos inside your mind. That chaos feels unsafe. You must either change your belief or do something to escape the chaos. Since so few of us have ever learned how to change a belief, we tend to go with the latter and try to escape the chaos. But escape only fixes our problems temporarily.

Operating By Default

Your mind is like an iceberg. The conscious mind comprises about five percent of your mind. It's only the tip you can see above water. Your unconscious mind is the ninety-five percent of the iceberg below the waterline of conscious awareness. Your unconscious mind works behind the scenes. It is literally doing a million things to keep you alive and well while you walk around experiencing life. Your conscious mind, on the other hand, can only manage about seven things at once (plus or minus two). It's a good thing that you don't have to remember to breathe while you are watching television. It's really great that you don't have to consciously digest your food or relearn how to walk every time you want to go somewhere. What an ingenious mind/body system! We spend the first eight to ten years of life loading up the 'software' that will help us to survive for the rest of our lives. Unfortunately, some of us uploaded some pretty crummy 'software' and until we upgrade it, we're going to be stuck operating from lousy perspectives.

Our intentions are created from our memories, our past references. If we have pain and trauma running our subconscious mind, then our intentions will likely involve elaborate ways to protect ourselves from what we perceive as the enemy including hiding, running, submitting, distracting, lashing out in anger, and, with severe trauma or PTSD, even kill or be killed.

Operating from emotional pain and trauma defines what it means to be a victim. The most effective way to step out of victimhood involves changing your past references. Yes, change your memories. When you change how you represent what has happened to you in the past, it changes your intentions. You can literally change your focus from anger to peace, from protection to creativity and from sadness to joy. You have that power within you right now. You always have.

Energy and action always follow thought. I used to believe that my thoughts were caused by what happened to me. If only someone had taught me as a child that my thoughts *caused* my actions, how different my life would have been. But there is no time like the present.

All your power is right here, right now. And you can begin to change your thoughts in the here-and-now. Change your default settings by changing the contents of your subconscious mind. What you focus on is what you receive. And, where your mind goes, your body follows. If your intention is to change some behavior and you are having trouble doing that, it's because your intention is focused on the wrong thing. Take your focus off the effect (the problem) and put it on the cause (what you hold within.) Once you clear the negative emotions, then you can begin to formulate a new intention for your life.

Workshop Of The Mind

FasterEFT tapping is a great mechanism for transforming emotional pain and trauma in your subconscious mind. Tapping gives you the ability to identify the root of your problems and restructure what you believe. However, once you have pulled out the negative, it is important to have a mechanism to load up the positive. You need to create the internal references for a new life you would love to live. You can do this by creating a workshop in your mind.

This idea was popularized by Napoleon Hill in his groundbreaking book, "Think and Grow Rich," back in the 1930s. Many of the extremely successful people he interviewed utilized some form of this technique. The most famous was the great inventor Thomas Edison. Edison used his daily "naps" as a mechanism for coming up with ideas. He called this process going to the "Land of Solutions." He would sit in a chair holding a small rock in his hand over a tin bucket. He wanted to be in a light trance, but not fully asleep. If he fell asleep, the rock would fall out of his hand and make a big noise in the tin bucket to wake him up.

Whenever he was stumped for an idea or solution, he would take one of his "naps" and come back an hour later with the information he needed.

Edison was accessing a Higher Intelligence, the same Higher Intelligence we all have access to. He found a way to connect, through his super-conscious mind, to his Higher Power. And so can you.

Your mind is structured in three parts. Your subconscious mind performs background tasks. Your conscious mind is free to think, plan, and execute. And your super conscious mind connects you to that ineffable, indescribable Source of All That Is. We are all connected to a creative Life Source. People call it God, Spirit, Universal Intelligence, Higher Power, First Cause and many other things. The life that animates your body comes from that Source. You are one with that and you are an extension of that. Your purpose in life is to be a unique expression of Source. You are here to be something that has never existed before and will never exist again exactly like you.

Consciously connecting to Source opens you up to unlimited resources you could never have imagined. When you try to do everything alone, you suffer. There is a Higher Power. And you can define It and utilize It as you see fit. That is how free will works. Your beliefs can limit your personal experience. But they cannot limit Source. Your Higher Power can only help and guide you to the extent that you invite It to help and guide you. You are free to experience freedom or bondage, limited or unlimited resources. Only you can choose.

If you are not accustomed to seeking information and guidance from your Higher Power, it may require some practice. Create some time every day to connect to this limitless Source. Intend to cultivate a relationship with your Higher Power. Because as you cultivate that relationship, your belief in It will grow and evidence will begin showing up for you. It's like any relationship. It deepens and becomes easier with time and effort.

Intention Plus Mechanism Equals Results

This psychological equation, originally expressed by Brian Klemmer, bestselling author and presenter of leadership training seminars, provides a real eye opener. When you are trying to manifest a particular result, how important is your intention and how important is the mechanism you use to acquire it? If Results equal one hundred percent, what percentage of intention (your emotional drive) and what percentage of mechanism (the how to) will take you to your goal? Think about it. Is it fifty percent intention plus fifty percent mechanism? Or do the scales lean more heavily to one side or the other? What do you think?

The first time I heard this, I was in a room full of people who all had different answers. I thought mine was pretty clever. I guessed ninety percent intention plus ten percent mechanism. I have been studying the power of the mind for a long time, so I thought I knew the answer. My workaholic friend, on the other hand, thought it had to be ten percent intention plus ninety percent mechanism. He was positive that success is all about hard work.

Want To Know The Answer?
In his seminars, Brian Klemmer presented his "Formula of Champions:"

100% Intention + 0% Mechanism = 100% Results.

Klemmer explained that if you are one hundred percent clear about your intention, and you couple it with an intense emotional desire, the mechanisms you need to accomplish it will begin to appear *automatically*. According to Klemmer, the number one reason people fail to accomplish what they want is a lack of clarity and strong intention. Indecision guarantees defeat. When you know exactly what you want and put passion and emotion behind your desire, you imagine yourself already at your goal. And, thoughts become things!

When Life feels the strength of your intention, it automatically opens doors that you did not even know existed. Things and people and circumstances begin showing up where before, there was nothing. When your intention is clear and strong, you naturally become committed. And when you are committed, you are unstoppable. Creating with intention involves trusting the flow of Life, trusting God, your Higher Power, and the Universe.

You are always committed to something. If you want to know what you are committed to, just look at your results. Look at what you have now. You say you want something better, but if you really wanted it with every aspect of your being, you would have it. Your subconscious mind is one hundred percent committed to the model of the world you currently have installed. The surest way to fire up your intention is to change your old model of the world which says you are a victim and you have to suffer. By changing how you internally represent your past, you change how you feel right now. And changing how you feel right now gives you the fuel to intend something new. A new intention will light a fire of commitment that will have a dramatic impact on what you are able to create in the future.

Commitment

Commitment is a loaded word. But what does it really mean? My friend and mentor, Lyla Messinger defines commitment as: "To be bound, responsible or obligated to a course of action or to a person or group that cannot be avoided." So what does it take to become all that?

Start By Getting Clear

The way you get clear about the present is to clean up your past. Then, you can make decisions from your true self, not from your childhood pains and hurts. Everything will look and feel different from your new, clear, powerful perspective.

Once you clear your old pain, your powerful mind opens up to all sorts of new possibilities. Maybe you will remember and reconnect to what you wanted to be as a child; that thing you shut out of your life because someone told you it was impossible for someone like you. Or, maybe you will decide to be something you never dreamed possible. Whatever it is, get excited about it. Set your intention. Light a flame that cannot be put out because it is who you are. You deserve to love your life!

STEP ELEVEN EXERCISES

Workshop of the Mind

Create a WORKSHOP in your mind. Some people call it their Happy Place. Others prefer to call it a workshop or laboratory.

- Make it real. Decorate it with furniture, a library, a computer, a movie screen, and a phone that goes straight to your Higher Power. Or maybe it's in a giant magical tree and you have an army of elves that help you. Use your imagination and create a safe and powerful place where you can go to work and get answers inside your mind. This is your Land of Solutions. It is the place where you make your deepest desires happen in thought first. Think of it as creating a spiritual prototype for what you will then create in your world.

- Formulate a new intention for your life. Don't worry about how it's going to happen or even if it's possible. Just create a positive intention for your future. If any negative thoughts arise, tap them away. Create a vision that brings you joy. Imagine how it will feel when that intention comes true.

- Spend time every day imagining yourself already being, doing and having whatever you intend. Make sure you have a strong positive feeling in your mind and in your body when you think about it.

- Remember, this is your dream. Keep it to yourself for a while. Seeds spend the first part of their life underground, in the dark. As long as you water and feed them and refrain from poisoning them, those seeds will germinate and begin to grow roots. Seeds grow down first, then when they have a strong enough foundation, they begins to grow up. Let your dream grow roots before you expose it to public opinion. Nurture it. Feed it every day inside your mind. Before you know it, it will grow tall enough that people will begin to notice. Protect it for as long as you can. Then, you will be prepared to blossom into your dream.

STEP TWELVE

LIVE WITH PASSION

The purpose of life is to discover your gift. The meaning of life is giving your gift away.

~David Viscott

The dictionary defines passion as "strong emotion" and "intense desire or enthusiasm."[12] But the root of the word passion comes from an ancient Latin word that means 'to suffer.' People refer to the suffering of Jesus as a "passion." How could the same word be related to both "intense desire and enthusiasm" and also "suffering?" It doesn't appear to make sense.

I recently heard Lance Miller, the Toastmasters World Champion of Public Speaking (2004), explain passion in a beautiful way:

Have you ever known a mom who complained about having to take her kids to soccer practice and piano lessons and get them a tutor to help with their school work? She is so overwhelmed and feels like she has lost herself in taking care of all her children's needs, while her needs are not met? This woman has lost her passion for being a mom. She is suffering.

And have you ever known a mom who was so excited to take her

---

12 New Oxford American Dictionary (Second Edition) App for Mac OS X, Version 10.9.5.

kids to practice and fix their lunches and drive them all over town? Whenever you ask her about her life, she launches into how great her children are doing. This woman is doing all the same things, but to her, it's a joy, not a pain. That's because she has not lost her passion for being a mom. She is engrossed in her passion, so the work is not a source of suffering.

What looks like suffering to some, is not suffering when passion is present. That's the difference.

When you have strong positive emotions, intense desire and enthusiasm, even if what you are doing is difficult, there is no suffering. How you internally represent whatever you are doing is the key to living a life you love.

Passion can be both a cause and an effect. In the same way that living from pain creates more pain, living with passion creates even more passion. And releasing your old hurts, sadness, fears, traumas, judgments, abandonments, betrayals, addictions, helplessness and everything else you do not want is almost like starting your life over. You clean the slate. Except, you are not a blank slate like you were when you were born.

You have accumulated wisdom over your lifetime. The best thing about releasing pain is that you get to keep the wisdom. Letting go is better than starting from scratch. You have gifts and talents that you might not have been able to see or use before. But now, your worst nightmare can actually become your greatest gift, if you let it. And I hope you do, because the world needs your gifts.

The Hero's Journey

Joseph Campbell describes the hero's journey in stages. The first stage is to hear a call and to answer it. There is reluctance at first. But once the hero sets out on the journey, s/he always meets a special mentor who offers supernatural aid. You don't make the hero's journey alone. There are always helpers and resources that you could never have imagined. The price you must pay to find these helpers and resources is commitment to the journey.

The most inspiring people I know are the ones who have been on a hero's journey and returned to tell the tale. Your life is a hero's journey, and you are the hero of your life. Others have gone before you and left clues about how to survive and thrive. When you take your own journey of releasing your painful past and begin to live your life with passion, you will become one of those hero guides.

The hero's journey sounds like a magical formula, and it is. When you commit yourself to healing yourself, your Higher Power will begin to materialize and work through people, places and things that you would never have otherwise imagined.

Creating a relationship with yourself is the first step in cultivating your relationship with your Higher Power because your Higher Power dwells within you. Your trials and ordeals may escalate as you progress, but each one will bring you wisdom, gifts and talents that you never imagined were possible. Yes, you! And just when you think it's not possible to succeed, you will learn to ask for help from within, as well as without. You will have acquired faith in yourself that will support you, and allow you to emerge victorious. You will become the master of your world and the master of your fate, which gives you the freedom to live with passion. Passion is power.

Take Back Your Power

Where are you now? Are you already on your healing journey? Or are you still reluctant to start? Perhaps this book is your call to a new journey. Your journey begins when you answer the call. If you want to take back your power, accept the challenge. Get inspired about your own personal transformation! And stop worrying about everyone else's. Recognize that your power does not reside in anyone else. No program, facility, healer, shaman, or priest has your answers or your power. Only you can heal you. You will have guides and allies along the way, but ultimately, everything you need is already within you. It has always been there. You may have been misguided as a child or had so much pain that you forgot who you were. But everything you need to live a joyful, passionate life is right inside you now. The best guides and helpers will always remind you to go within.

Reverend Michael Beckwith, New Thought spiritual leader, author, and star of the movie *The Secret* once said "You cannot hide your secret thoughts because they show up as your life." Recognize the powerful tool you have inside and begin to use it wisely. There is no cavalry coming to save you. You are the cavalry. You are One with the Power and Presence that created you. You live in It and It lives in you. It's time to recognize and remember your wholeness with your Source.

Get Connected To Source

New Thought philosophy describes the nature of who and what you are in an elegant way. Source (God, Spirit, Higher Power, Infinite Intelligence or whatever name you give it) encompasses all that is, both the seen and the unseen; the visible and the invisible. Beyond all ability for humans to comprehend, every person, place, thing and situation is an expression of that infinite, ever expanding Source. And that includes you!

This infinite creative Source has only one way to know Itself and that is to continuously expand and express Itself as the infinite variety of Life all around us. In the invisible, undifferentiated realm, there is no judgment; no good or bad. Life simply is. It exists. It expresses infinite uniqueness, all the time. Everything in existence is Life expressing Itself in infinite variety. When you acknowledge that you are a part of this divine process, you realize that you are a center of divine action.

Your job in life is to express your uniqueness. So if you have been trying to fit into someone else's mold (or resist someone else's idea of what you should be) your whole life, now you know why that isn't working for you. You were never meant to be like anyone except you. You are a magnificent creation put here to express your uniqueness. Embrace that thought!

Universal and Individual

The Universal aspect of life is forever giving, expanding and expressing. The purpose of an individual life is to direct that Universal expression in unique ways. There has never been anyone exactly like you and there never will be. You are a unique expression of the divine Source of all that is. Life is your gift from Source and your participation with life — how you direct it and what you choose to create with it — is your gift back to Life. Life cannot do anything for you or to you. It can only operate *through* you. Like water flowing through a pipe, it takes the shape and direction of the thing that directs it.

Life is an infinite unformed substance. Your every thought, every mental image and every word directs this highly sensitive unformed substance into material form. Your mind is a powerful center through which the creative process operates. The only reason your wishes do not materialize is because they are not your dominant thoughts and pictures. You may occasionally wish for better health or freedom from addiction or more money. But if you examine the exact nature of your thoughts and feelings—the ones that run through your mind for an entire day, week, month, or decade, you will find that they are in opposition to what you say you want.

The good news is, with a little effort, anyone can transform their thoughts from one form to another. As you practice using your power deliberately (as it was intended), instead of accidentally or by default, you will begin to build proof and belief in this simple truth: that you are a center of divine distribution. The one creative Power and Presence that exists brought you into form for the purpose of expanding and enjoying Itself through you and as you. Your thoughts give It direction and purpose. You are not a victim. You are more powerful than you know. The things you want most—love, acceptance, joy, freedom, beauty, connection, significance, or anything else—want you. Your dream is already inside you, waiting to be recognized and developed. Your good is a natural part of who you already are. When you take control of the contents of your mind, no thing and no person can prevent you from creating and having whatever you desire. Your life is in your hands now.

What Is Real?

The only thing that is truly real is this moment, right now. The past was real when it was happening, but it's over now. The past is no longer real unless you drag it into the present and use your mind and body to create the same feelings you had in the past in this now moment. Let the past go so you can use this powerful now moment to create something new. You can use this now moment to create your heart's desire or to re-create the past. The choice is yours.

What is real is that you are one with your Higher Power. Your Higher Power, however you want to name it, is not something that lives in the sky or in a special building or individual. God made you so that It can express Its limitless nature in, through and as you. It does not matter what has happened in the past. You may still have to deal with some effects that your old behaviors or experiences set into motion, but even they will eventually pass. You can choose to release the pain in your past and embrace a new way of being right now and in every subsequent moment. You can choose peace, joy, forgiveness, healing and passion.

You cannot be passionate in the past or in the future. In fact, you cannot *be* in the past or the future. It's not possible. The only thing that exists is right now; the present. My question to you is, who are you being right now? What qualities are you using to create your life? Are you being courageous or helpless? Are you being compassionate or disruptive? Who and what would you rather be? Passion is a quality of being you can choose.

Be Present

The journey to living with passion involves being mindful of how you *feel* in every moment. Notice in every moment if you are feeling good or not good. If you are feeling good, amplify it. Write it down in your Happy Journal so you can remember it when you need to feel better. If you are feeling something unpleasant, notice what it is and then tap until you feel peace and freedom. It's a never-ending process. But you will, over time, clear so many negative triggers that you will begin to live life with less pain and more joy. Your new normal will become peace and passion. You will find yourself moving toward things that make you feel good, and you will naturally encounter less and less of the things that make you feel bad.

You deserve to feel good, no matter what. In fact, it is important for you to feel good. I believe if everyone on the planet would take ownership of how they feel and begin to practice emotional intelligence, we would realize world peace. Peace begins inside you and inside me. Let's take this journey together and create a world of peace, beauty, love and passion.

STEP TWELVE EXERCISES

Practice Presence
The practice of being present is often referred to as mindfulness. Everything you think, say and do impacts both you and the people and environment around you. Hypervigilance is not necessary. There is no need to create extra stress for yourself. Begin simply.
- Practice being aware of the triggers that send you rushing down a path of pain. Notice them for a moment. Allow yourself to actually feel your feelings without running for your escape mechanism. As you allow yourself to feel the fear or craving or anger without judging or acting on it, you will begin to notice that it eventually moves on. Mindfulness can make you fearless. It eventually brings peace because nothing in life comes to stay. Everything comes to pass.

Practice Passion
Find what you want your life to stand for and immerse yourself in that. Your passion will take you to new levels and it may even heal the world.

ACKNOWLEDGEMENTS

First and foremost, I recognize that One Power and Presence that I call God as my Source. I have often heard people say that writing is a solitary business. And it is. However, the simple act of putting pen to paper — or fingers to keyboard — has become my way to open to an inner conversation with the Ineffable. I am so grateful for that feeling of connection and wholeness that I receive when I am writing.

Now, getting me to take time and make the effort to sit down and write has involved the love and support of some very special people. Early support came from my spiritual community at the Center for Spiritual Living Orange County. Reverends Sandy and Kirk Moore provided me with steady encouragement. Sandy and Kirk, I am deeply inspired by your dedication to the spiritual path and your sincere and loving guidance. How wonderful it is to watch you both walk your talk with such dedication and consistency. You gave me courage to take my idea and begin to sculpt it into something resembling a book. Your support and encouragement throughout the process has been unwavering, even giving me a place to present workshops and to offer tapping sessions. I am so blessed to have you both in my life!

The quality of my life would be very different if I had never met and studied with Robert G. Smith, creator of FasterEFT. This book would not exist if I had not been able to transform the deeply embedded subconscious programming that kept me playing small for most of my life. I am so grateful for the FasterEFT style of tapping. Tapping has changed my life in so many ways and it has empowered me to help others to make big changes. Robert, I am so blessed that you created not only this amazing skill, but also a loving and supportive community. Thank you for welcoming me into your FasterEFT family. I am especially grateful for the opportunity to serve with Robert Smith along with other advanced practitioners at the Habilitat long term drug and alcohol treatment facility, where I got to practice the FasterEFT Addiction Protocol. How exciting to witness real people letting go of serious addictions as they released the painful emotional drivers that caused their problems in the first place. Robert, I am humbled by your dedication and compassion for people who are suffering. You change lives wherever you go and you inspire me every day. The world is a better place because you are in it. God bless you, Robert.

When it was time to get serious about completing my manuscript, my Chi Camp buddies, Rita Duncan and Andrea Daniels kept me on track with strict accountability to my self imposed deadlines. I might still be stuck in the middle without you. I am especially grateful to Andrea and Rita for trusting me as a FasterEFT practitioner, allowing me the honor of helping them to create some big life changes. You both inspire me. And what a joy to watch Rita very quickly grow into an awesome practitioner who is now helping me! Love you, Buddy!

And to my Chi Camp guides, Lyla Messinger and Janet Henze, thank you so much for helping me to gain a sense of urgency as well as a deeper commitment to personal integrity. You are amazing teachers who practice what you preach.

To my friend and mentor, Leonard Szymczak — writing coach extraordinaire — I am so grateful to be one of your "book babies." Your guidance and support through the editing process has been invaluable. You are single handedly responsible for taking my writing up several notches and I cannot thank you enough! In weeks, I learned more about style, structure and "the current rules" of writing in a professional manner than I could have learned in a year of study on my own.

I also need to thank Leonard for introducing me to my cover designer, Fiona Jayde, and my book's interior designer, Tamara Cribley. Thank you Fiona for your amazing artistic ability as well as your grounding in what actually sells. And Tamara, thank you for giving my book the professional, polished look and feel I was hoping for. You both made the finishing touches beautiful, effortless and professional.

For my early reviewers, Susie Shecter, Dr. Cheryl Cuttineau, Joanie Newman, Karen Clay, Bill Condon, Anna-Becky Redlich, and Kim Jewell. I am so grateful for your time and loving support. The feedback you provided was priceless and helped me to shape parts of my book in ways I could never have done without your valuable comments and suggestions.

I am deeply grateful to all of my FasterEFT clients. Each and every one has brought me to a deeper level of compassion and non-judgment, both for others and for myself. In every session, I get to witness how easy it can be for anyone to let go of old painful memories and behaviors and to create new mental resources that automatically change their life! My client's courage and willingness to take control of their perceptions and create freedom, health and prosperity where there was a lack of it inspires me and reminds me that my life is as fantastic as I allow it to be.

I am so blessed to have amazing siblings who have supported and inspired me through my writing process. My sister, Anna-Becky Redlich, has been my closest friend and confidant since birth. Her reckless generosity, fierce love and willingness to stand up for what she believes in inspires me daily. My sister Shirley Condon operates from a level of loving kindness that, at times, borders on sainthood. My brother Bill Condon is a model of intelligence, kindness, fun and authenticity. I am so grateful for the unique feedback and input from each of you.

And finally, to my beloved husband, Dovell Bonnett, thank you for your love, kindness and incredible support throughout this process. You are my rock!

RESOURCE GUIDE

For a full length seminar video about tapping on addictions, visit the link below to watch Robert Smith teaching at Habilitat, a long term residential drug and alcohol treatment center in Hawaii:
http://www.youtube.com/watch?v=JBA5HJqcTa0

For additional resources or to contact me personally, please visit my website: www.FasterEFTworks.com

For a dose of inspiration, visit my blog:
www.12NewSteps.com

For tap along videos, visit my website or Robert Smith's YouTube Channel: www.YouTube.com/HealingMagic

To attend a workshop or to get trained in FasterEFT, visit Robert Smith's website: www.FasterEFT.com/Events

To find a FasterEFT Practitioner (worldwide), go to:
www.FasterEFT.com/practitioner-directory

BIBLIOGRAPHY

(In alphabetical order)

Allen, James. *As A Man Thinketh*. New York: Grosset & Dunlap/Putnam Publishing Group, 2006.

Beckwith, Michael Bernard. *Spiritual Liberation: Fulfilling Your Soul's Potential*. New York: Atria Books/Beyond Words, 2008.

Behrend, Genevieve. *Your Invisible Power: A Presentation of the Mental Science of Thomas Troward*. Camarillo: DeVorss Publications, 1951.

Blume, W.T. *Atlas of Pediatric Encephalography*. New York: Raven Press, 1982.

Bodenhamer, Bob G. and Hall, Michael L. *The User's Manual for the Brain: The Complete Manual for Neuro-Linguistic Programming Practitioner Certification, Volume 1*. Bethel: Crown House Publishing Company LLC, 2009.

Byrne, Rhonda. *The Secret*. New York: Atria Books, 2006.

Cameron, Julia. *The Artist's Way: A Spiritual Path to Higher Creativity, 10th Anniversary Edition*. New York: Jeremy P. Tarcher/Putnam, 2002.

Campbell, Joseph. *Hero with A Thousand Faces*. New York: MJF Books, 1949.

Chopra, Deepak. *Creating Health*. New York: Houghton Mifflin Company, 1991.

Cohen, Andrew. *Evolutionary Enlightenment: A New Path to Spiritual Awakening.* New York: Select Books, Inc., 2011.

Cope, Stephen. *The Great Work of Your Life: A Guide for the Journey to Your True Calling.* New York: Bantam Books, 2012.

Dispenza, Joe. *You Are The Placebo: Making Your Mind Matter.* Carlsbad: Hay House, Inc., 2014.

Dyer, Wayne W. *Wishes Fulfilled: Mastering the Art of Manifesting.* Carlsbad: Hay House, Inc., 2012.

Eker, T. Harv. *Secrets of the Millionaire Mind: Mastering the Inner Game of Wealth.* New York: Harper Business, 2005.

Elman, Dave. *Hypnotherapy.* Glendale: Westwood Publishing Company, 1964.

Emerson, Ralph Waldo. *Emerson's Essays.* New York: Thomas Y. Crowell Company, Inc., 1926.

Goldsmith, Joel S. *Practicing the Presence: The Inspirational Guide to Regaining Meaning and A Sense of Purpose in Your Life.* New York: Harper Collins, 1958.

Goldsmith, Joel S. *The Foundation of Mysticism: Spiritual Healing Principles of the Infinite Way.* Acropolis Books, Inc., 1998.

Harris, Bill. *Thresholds of the Mind: Your Personal Roadmap to Success, Happiness and Contentment.* Beverton: Centerpointe Research Institute, Inc., 2007.

Hawkins, David. *Power vs. Force: The Hidden Determinates of Human Behavior.* Carlsbad: Hay House, Inc., 2002.

Hay, Louise L. *You Can Heal Your Life.* Carlsbad: Hay House, Inc., 1984.

Heller, Steven and Steele, Terry. *Monsters and Magical Sticks: There's No Such Thing As Hypnosis?* Tempe: The Original Falcon Press, 2009.

Hicks, Esther and Jerry. *Ask and It Is Given.* Carlsbad: Hay House, Inc., 2004.

Hill, Napoleon. *Think and Grow Rich.* North Hollywood: Wilshire Book Publishing, 1966.

Holmes, Ernest. *Living the Science of Mind.* Camarillo: DeVorss & Company, 1984.

Holmes, Ernest. *The Science of Mind: A Philosophy, A Faith, A Way of Life.* New York: Jeremy P. Tarcher/Putnam, 1938.

Jewell, Kim J. *From Stress to Success: Faster Emotionally Focused Transformation.* Kim J. Jewell, 2012.

Linden, Anné. *Mindworks: An Introduction to NLP, The Secrets of Your Mind Revealed.* Bethel: Crown House Publishing Company, LLC, 2011.

McBride, Terry. *The Hell I Can't.* Mesa: McBride Enterprises, 2003.

Moore, Kirk. *Tara's Angels: One Family's Extraordinary Journey of Courage and Healing.* Irvine: Opa Publishing, 2003.

Moore, Sandy and Moore, Deanna. *The Green Intention: Living in Sustainable Joy.* Camarillo: DeVorss & Company, 2011.

Moore, Thomas. *Care of the Soul: A Guide for Cultivating Depth and Sacredness in Everyday Life.* New York: Harper Collins Publishers, 1992.

Moorjani, Anita. *Dying To Be Me: A Journey from Cancer to Near Death to True Healing.* Carlsbad: Hay House, Inc., 2012.

Nichols, Lisa. *No Matter What: 9 Steps to Living the Life You Love.* New York: Wellness Central, 2009.

Peirce, Penney. *Frequency: The Power of Personal Vibration.* New York: Atria Books/Beyond Words Publishing, 2009.

Ponder, Catherine. *The Dynamic Laws of Healing.* Marina Del Rey: DeVorss, 1966.

Rankin, Lissa. *Mind Over Medicine: Scientific Proof You Can Heal Yourself.* Carlsbad: Hay House, Inc., 2013

Segal, Inna. *The Secret Language of Your Body: The Essential Guide to Health and Wellness.* New York: Atria Books/Beyond Words Paperback Edition, 2010.

Shimoff, Marci. *Happy for No Reason: 7 Steps to Being Happy from the Inside Out.* New York: Free Press, 2008.

Szymczak, Leonard. *The Roadmap Home: Your GPS to Inner Peace.* Leonard Szymczak, 2009.

Tolle, Eckhart. *A New Earth: Awakening to Your Life's Purpose.* New York: Dutton/Penguin Group (USA), Inc., 2005.

Williamson, Marianne. *A Return to Love.* New York: Harper Collins, 1992.

Williamson, Marianne. *The Gift of Change: Spiritual Guidance for A Radically New Life.* New York: Harper Collins e-books, 2009.

Zukav, Gary. *The Seat of the Soul.* New York: Fireside, 1989.

ABOUT THE AUTHOR

Marguerite Bonnett is an advanced FasterEFT practitioner dedicated to helping people transform their lives. Her unique style of tapping focuses on finding and breaking through old subconscious behaviors and changing outcomes. Her recent work with the FasterEFT Tapping Marathon at Habilitat Drug and Alcohol Treatment Program in Hawaii, the number one rehab in America, proved to her that addicts do not have to feel hopeless because addictions can be eliminated.

Marguerite operates from the belief that there are no broken people, only people operating from broken and hurt ideas, which they may not even realize they have. She knows from experience that the fastest and best way to make real and lasting change is to make peace with the past and to actually install new beliefs about what is possible for the future.

Marguerite draws on her rich experiential background to bring a down to Earth practicality to her teaching and her work. Most of her life has been dedicated to studying with modern masters of healing and transformation. She learned to meditate at the age of fourteen and a year later began studying Jose Silva's Mind Control program. Since then, she has studied extensively with Anthony Robbins (yes, she walked barefoot across hot coals without getting burned!), Bob Proctor, Barbara DeAngelis, Mary Morrissey, Jean Houston and many others.

As a graduate of the Berkeley Psychic Institute, Marguerite went on to teach Women's Intuition and Energy Healing techniques at their Silicon Valley campus. She is a Religious Science Licensed Prayer Practitioner, a Master Practitioner of Neuro Linguistic Programming (NLP), and a certified Hypnotherapist. Marguerite is also an inspirational speaker and artist. Marguerite lives in Orange County, California with her husband and her rescued Rottweiler, Dori.

www.FasterEFTworks.com

Made in the USA
San Bernardino, CA
07 August 2015